Roots of
The
Islamic
Revolution
in Iran

Roots of THE ISLAMIC REVOLUTION

in Iran

Four lectures by Hamid Algar
Revised and Expanded Edition

iPi
Oneonta, New York

Published and distributed by
Islamic Publications International
P.O Box 705, Oneonta, NY 13820. USA
Telephone: 800-568-9814   Fax: 800-466-8111
Email: Islampub@Islampub.com

First Revised Edition 2001
        Algar, Hamid
            Roots of the Islamic revolution in Iran: four lectures/
        by Hamid Algar -- Rev. and expanded ed.
            p. cm.
            Includes bibliographical references and index.
            LCCN: 2001132785
            ISBN: 1-889999-26-1 (paperback)
            ISBN: 1-889999-27-X (hardback)

            1. Islam and politics--Iran. 2. Iran -- Politics and
        government -- 1941-1979. I. Title

        BP63.I68A37 2001   322.4'2'0882971
                                  QBI01-200489

Director of Publications: Moin Shaikh
Book Design & Composition: Sharon Okada
Indexer: Katherine Jensen
Editor: Jane Merryman

In Memory of
Dr. Kalim Siddiqui

Contents

𐤀𐤁𐤂𐤃𐤄

Introduction

الله أكبر الله ولا إله إلا الله

R evisiting words written or spoken in the fairly distant past -
- in the present case, more than twenty years after the event
-- can be a sobering experience. All too often, the passage of
time will be seen to have laid bare hasty or superficial judgements;
provided alert readers with ample opportunity to focus eagerly on
factual errors, major or minor; and mercilessly belied predictions,
implicit or explicit, once made with rash and unseemly confidence. The temptation to undertake a thorough revision in order
to efface all possible cause for embarrassment is strong.

The urge is particularly great, although resistible, in the present case, for this is almost the first time I have been able to take
editorial control of the text of four modest and extemporaneous
lectures I delivered in London in the summer of 1979. With a single exception, none of those who subsequently published or translated the lectures communicated with me before going to press.
They were first published in 1980 under the title *The Islamic
Revolution in Iran* as a cyclostyled brochure by *al-marhum* Kalim
Siddiqui, at whose invitation they were delivered at the Muslim
Institute in London. They were then reprinted in book form,
under the title *Roots of the Islamic Revolution*, by the Open Press in
1983, again by Kalim Siddiqui, who this time contributed a foreword and a preface. At a date unknown, Ansariyan Publishers of
Qum -- who are quite possibly the most voracious violators of
copyright in the world, at least of Islamic books -- produced
another English edition, with no mention of the author's name,
and the third chapter entirely excised, presumably because of their

disapproval of Shari'ati. The book was twice translated into Persian, once by the Sipah-i Pasdaran-i Inqilab-i Islami (The Corps of Guards of the Islamic Revolution), probably in 1980, and once by Murtaza As'adi and Hasan Chizari in 1981.[1] The text of the second lecture appeared in Indonesian translation in 1984.[2] A Turkish version, prepared by M. Çetin Demirhan, appeared in Istanbul in 1988.[3] The book is also reported to have been translated into Bengali, although no copy has ever reached my hands. A French translation of extracts from the lectures, duly reviewed by myself, appeared in the review *le débat* in 1981.[4]

This history of publication testifies not so much to the excellence or profundity of the text, as to the paucity of informed reportage and analysis of the Islamic Republic, particularly during its early years, and the interest and enthusiasm it generated among many Muslims who were anxious to learn something of its historical roots. At a time when the revolution was being widely depicted as a misguided affair of mass retrograde confusion, bound to collapse in the face of internal division and leftist intrigue, my presentation of a few simple and positive facts concerning its nature, origins, and rooting in Iranian history, was experienced by many as a welcome and reassuring corrective. Particularly in the revised form now being presented to the reader, these lectures may still serve as a useful summary description of the forces that led to revolution and the historical background of that signal event.

---

[1] *Iran va Inqilab-i Islami*, Tehran: Intisharat-i Sipah-i Pasdaran-i Inqilab-i Islami, n.d.; *Inqilab-i Islami dar Iran*, Tehran: Intisharat-i Qalam, 1360 Sh./1981. Neither of the translations was free of error, although both were accompanied by criticisms of some of my statements, justifiably in a few cases.

[2] "Khomeini Penjelmaan Sebuah Tradisi," in *Gerbang Kebangkitan: Revolusi Islam dan Khomeini dalam Perbincangan*, Yogyakarta: Shalahuddin Press, 1984, pp. 203-249.

[3] *Islam Devriminin Kokleri*, Istanbul: Isaret Yayinlari, 1988.

[4] "Sources et figures de la revolution islamique en Iran," *le débat*, 14 (July-August, 1981), pp. 54-76. The same extracts were reprinted in Pierre Nora, ed., *Islam et politique au proche-orient*, Paris: Gallimard, 1991, pp. 210-255.

I have taken advantage of the opportunity afforded by this republication to make corrections of fact and modifications of judgement, sometimes in the text and sometimes in the form of footnotes. Some of these changes I would have made twenty years ago, if the transcript of my lectures had been forwarded to me for revision in advance of publication; others derive from the corrective notes appended to the Persian translations mentioned above; and still others have been suggested by the passage of time and the course of events. I have retained, although in some cases modified, the text of the question and answer sessions that followed each lecture, for they, like the lectures themselves, reflect the anxieties, hopes and uncertainties present in many minds during those early months. On the other hand, I have suppressed the names of those posing the questions, for they may not wish to remain permanently linked to queries and observations spontaneously made two decades ago. Exception is made only of Kalim Siddiqui, who organised the lectures and chaired the sessions at which they were presented. I have also taken the liberty of curtailing the laudatory remarks with which he closed the final session.

Throughout the text I have substituted the title "Imam" for "Ayatullah" when referring to the leader of the Islamic Revolution as a more adequate indication of the role that he played (for the precise significance of the title as applied to him, see p. 78).

The title *Roots of the Islamic Revolution*, given to the second English edition and reflected in the Turkish translation, was chosen by Kalim Siddiqui; if I had been consulted on the matter, I would have opted for something more modest. It goes without saying that the "roots" of so complex a phenomenon as a revolution, insofar as they are discernible, cannot be adequately identified in a little more than one hundred pages. I have nonetheless decided to retain the title in order to prevent the impression that the present book is an entirely original work. The choice of title is, moreover, marginally defensible in that the book can count as a preliminary essay in uncovering those roots.

Finally, I have supplemented the work with fresh translations from the writings both of Imam Khomeini and of Dr. Shari'ati.

Although illustrating the difference in tone and depth of under-standing between the two personalities, these translations also suggest the urgent desire for Islamically-inspired change that was common to both of them and provided the motive force for that greatest event of contemporary Islamic history, the Islamic Revolution of Iran.

Hamid Algar
Berkeley, Dhu'l Qia'da 1421/February 2001

Iran and Shiʻism

The subject of the Islamic Revolution in Iran is one whose importance hardly needs underlining. With the passage of time, its importance will become even clearer as being the most significant and profound event in the entirety of contemporary Islamic history. Already we see the impact of the Islamic Revolution manifested in different ways and different degrees across the length and breadth of the Islamic world, from Morocco to Indonesia, from Bosnia in the heart of Europe down to Africa.

It is not surprising that in the face of the wave of renewal that has been at least partly inaugurated by the Iranian Islamic Revolution, the holders of power in the Islamic world, not to mention their various agents and representatives abroad, are seeking to contain the effect of the Islamic Revolution within the boundaries of Iran. They also seek to suggest that the Islamic Revolution has certain particular characteristics that do not permit of an extension beyond Iran. The easiest and most obvious way in which they attempt to accomplish this task is by branding the movement in Iran as a Shiʻi movement and Shiʻi in a divisive and exclusive sense. I do not wish to give the impression that through choosing the title for the first lecture of "Iran and Shiʻism," I am in any way contributing, even unintentionally, to this campaign for putting a particular and limiting stamp on the Islamic Revolution. It is, nonetheless, the case that from a historical point of view, the Revolution in Iran and the foundation of the Islamic Republic is the culmination of a series of events that began in the sixteenth century of the Christian era with the adherence of the majority of the Iranian people to the Shi'i school of thought in Islam. Indeed, one of the important factors that sets the Islamic Revolution apart from other revolutionary upheavals of the present century is its deep roots in the historical past.

Whereas the Russian, Chinese, and other revolutions, at least in theory, seek to negate the past in a radical fashion, to react against it, on the contrary, the Islamic Revolution is the continuation, the culmination of an important part of the Islamic heritage of Iran. In one sense the beginning of that heritage comes with the introduction of Islam to Iran in the seventh century of the Christian era. In a more immediate and important sense, the appropriate point of departure for our examination of the historical background of the Revolution is the early part of the sixteenth century, which sees the conversion of Iran into the only country in the Muslim world with a majority adhering to the Shi'i school of thought. It is appropriate, therefore, also to say at least a few words about Shi'ism.

The Shi'i school of thought in Islam, which has an extremely complex history, has gone through many different stages of development, both in Iran and outside. It is hardly possible for me to attempt even a sketch of those developments here. What I will lay emphasis upon are those aspects within the context of Iran that have had an important political and social impact. Whatever version of Shi'ism one looks at, at whatever point it may have expressed itself in Islamic history, the crucial point has been the doctrine of the Imamate, the figure of the Imam, who is not merely the successor of the Prophet (on whom and whose family be peace) in a legislative, administrative, and even military capacity, but also represents in some sense an extension of the spiritual dimensions of the prophetic mission. Let there be no mistake: Shi'i Muslims, like the Sunnis, fully accept and believe in the sealing of prophethood with the Prophet Muhammad (on whom and whose family be peace). However, they differ in their theory of the succession, not merely in the identity of the successor, but also in the functions of the successor. The functions of the successor, the Imam, in Shi'i beliefs, include the authoritative explanation of the

text of the Qur'an, the authoritative interpretation and even extension of Islamic law, the guidance of the individual in his spiritual
life in a fashion somewhat akin to the role of the *murshid* in
Sufism, and the role of sole legitimate leader of the entire Muslim
community -- the *ummah*.

Given the occultation, the *ghaiba* of the Imam (that is, his disappearance, his absence from the plane of physical history from
the 3rd/9th century), it can be said that in a certain sense much
that is implied in the Shi'i doctrine of the Imam has also absented
itself from the worldly plane. This absence of the Imam has been
one of the constant preoccupations of Shi'i philosophy, mysticism
and, speculation. What we are concerned with here is chiefly its
political implications. If the sole legitimate successor of the
Prophet, if the sole wielder of legitimate authority after him is no
longer present on the earthly plane, that means that inherently any
worldly power that claims to exercise authority must *ipso facto* be
illegitimate unless it can demonstrate in a clear and indisputable
fashion that it exercises rule on behalf of the absent Imam. This
very important belief has led the Shi'i Muslims to assume
throughout the major part of their history a stance of rejection or
at best limited acquiescence with regard to political authority, with
regard to *de facto* existing political authority; whereas for the
greater part of the history of the Sunni Muslims the prevailing
political theory, in its classical formulation by al-Mawardi, was
that the existing political power should not be disputed on condition that a few simple preconditions were observed, like the sultan
performing the Friday prayer and the *shari'a*, at least certain segments of the *shari'a*, being formally implemented.

Whereas this was the predominant theory of the Sunni
Muslims, and we see traces of it even today in the Sunni Muslim
countries, Shi'is often rejected the notion of an accommodation
with the existing political system. This rejection was sometimes
purely theoretical, and in fact its practical implications had not
been fully worked out and realized in the case of Iran right now
until the Islamic Revolution itself, which, one can see, is the final
implementation, or the logical implementation, of the political

theory of Shi'ism. In any event, it has been present as a powerful attitude throughout the history of the Shi'i school of thought in Islam and most particularly in Iran.

Another theme of Shi'ism in general that we may refer to before passing on to the particular case of Iran, is the importance given to the concept of martyrdom. Martyrdom is not in any way a monopoly concern of the Shi'a. It is a common value of all Muslims, having its archetype in the example given by certain Companions of the Prophet (upon whom and whose family be peace). Nonetheless, it has acquired a certain particular flavor and importance in the context of Shi'ism. This has been through the martyrdom of Imam Husain who, we can say, after the Prophet (upon whom and whose family be peace) and after Hazrat Ali (upon whom be peace) the first Imam is doubtless the most important figure in the religious consciousness of the Shi'a. The fact that he met his death in battle, that he attained martyrdom, is seen by the Shi'a not simply as a fact of history; it is seen as a fact of profound and continuing spiritual significance. In the person of Imam Husain (upon whom be peace) the whole fate of humanity when faced with overwhelming and tyrannical power is seen to have crystallized in a single significant incident, and the commemoration of this incident year after year is not merely a matter of pietistic commemoration. It is not a question of remembering a certain event in human history; it is, at least implicitly, a self-identification with Imam Husain and the determination to participate to some degree, through emotion and intention, with Imam Husain (upon whom be peace) in a struggle for justice against the overwhelming powers of tyranny. In the course of the Revolution in Iran one of the interesting slogans that was constantly raised, and which shows clearly the importance of Imam Husain not only for the religious but the political consciousness of the Shi'a, was: "Every day is Ashura, and every place is Karbala." In other words, wherever the Muslim is, is a field of struggle where the forces of justice and legitimacy are confronted by the forces of tyranny. Every day of his life is a day of battle in which he should seek either triumph or martyrdom. In addition to the important theme of the absence of the legitimate political authority, the refusal to bow before the existing political authority in the name of public order, joined to this we have an important contribution with the concept of martyrdom, as exemplified in particularly tragic and significant fashion by Imam Husain (upon whom be peace).

The combination of these two themes, the rejection of *de facto* authority and the belief in the virtue of martyrdom, has given Shi'ism, particularly at certain points in its history, an attitude of militancy that has been sadly lacking in a large number of Sunni segments of the Muslim Ummah. To summarize it and to quote yet another slogan of the Revolution in Iran, it has been said that the *mihrab* (prayer-niche) of the Shi'a is a *mihrab* of blood. That is, throughout the history of the Shi'a, in their confrontation with the powers of illegitimacy, they have been pushed to martyrdom and to self-sacrifice.

Let us pass to the particular case of Iran and the historical circumstances of the emergence of Shi'ism in Iran. Shi'ism, which today appears closely mingled with the whole Iranian sense of national identity, was in its origins almost entirely a stranger to Iran. Among the various Orientalist theories that have been elaborated with respect to the origins of Shi'ism it has been said that this was the Iranian response to an "Arab Islam." Apart from the inappropriateness of these ethnic categories, there is the simple fact that the earliest Shi'is were themselves, with few exceptions, Arabs, and Iran was for a long time an overwhelmingly Sunni country. Aside from a few centers, traditional centers such as Qum, which we shall hear more about later, and various quarters of other major cities, Shi'ism was little represented in Iran. In the aftermath of the Mongol conquest of the Muslim Near East in the thirteenth century, when the authority of the Abbasid Caliphate was shattered and destroyed, with the consequent weakening at least in the official position of Sunni thought, a gradual increase in the influence of Shi'ism in Iran began to be noticed. The stages of this are difficult to delineate completely and in any event the process was by no means a rapid and irreversible one. On the very eve of the conversion of Iran to Shi'ism, at the beginning of the tenth/sixteenth century, we find that Iran was still an overwhelmingly Sunni country. Strangely enough, despite the fact that within a short period of time a close mingling of Iranian national identity and Shi'ism had taken place, we find that there are two external factors that were crucial for the implantation of Shi'ism in Iran.

The first was the Safavid dynasty (1502-1722), originally a Turkish speaking family of hereditary Sufi shaykhs centered in the northwestern frontier lands of Iran. Transforming itself into a contender for power, it recruited a large number of followers from outside Iran from the Turkic nomads of Asia Minor, Syria, and the southern Caucasus. Afterwards the Safavids for political reasons manufactured a false genealogy for themselves, seeking descent from Imam Musa Kazim, the seventh Imam of the Prophets Family (peace be upon him). Subsequently, historical research has shown this genealogy to be false and that on the contrary they are of Turkic and ultimately Kurdish descent. In any event, the military forces that brought the Safavids to power in Iran were mostly non-Iranian and recruited from outside Iran.

We may even think of the foundation of the Safavid state in Iran as being in many ways one more nomadic invasion of this country, with this difference, that unlike the Mongol invasion, it came not from the east but from the west. After these Turkic nomads had placed the Safavids on the throne of Iran and the decision had been made to convert the majority of the people, if necessary by force, to Shi'ism, it was found that there were barely any Shi'i scholars in Iran and very few books available on Shi'ism in the Persian language. Consequently there took place the second influx of an external element, on this occasion Shi'i Arab scholars from traditional centers of Shi'ism in the Arab world, that is to say, Bahrain and Al-Ahsa in the Arabian Peninsula and Jabal 'Amil in the southern part of Syria.

These scholars were at the origin of the class of Iranian *ulama* that we have seen assuming a progressively more important historical role through the centuries until the culmination of that tradition in the Islamic Revolution. Despite this reliance on two external elements for the propagation of Shi'ism in Iran, the Turkic soldiery and Arab scholars, we see that in some fashion the ground must have been very well prepared. Historical research is not yet in a position to tell us how precisely this preparation took place. It is clear that for any spiritual tradition to flourish and take root, the mere process of coercion will not be sufficient. Although the Safavids did engage freely in the use of coercion leading to a large stream of emigration from Iran to neighboring Sunni countries, nonetheless, in a few generations Shi'ism had not only taken root in Iran, it had begun to produce one of the major intellectual and cultural flowering of the Islamic tradition as a whole. For this to have taken place, clearly the ground must have been prepared. Shi'ism found a suitable environment to flourish in Iran.

I turn now, within the context of this general development of Shi'ism in Iran, to the emergence of this class of Shi'i *ulama*. With the hindsight provided by the Islamic Revolution it might be more appropriate to write the Iranian history of the past four or five centuries not so much in terms of dynasties as in terms of the development of the class of the Iranian *ulama*. Dynasties have come and gone, leaving in many cases little more than a few artifacts behind to testify to their existence. But there has been a continuing development of the class of Shi'i *ulama* in Iran that has been largely without parallel elsewhere in the Islamic world. The origins of the Iranian Shi'i *ulama* are with those scholars imported by the Safavids from various Arab countries. Given the fact that they were often dependent on royal patronage, they were initially obedient and loyal servants of the state. One finds one of the earliest among them, for example, a certain Shaykh 'Ali Karaki, even writing a treatise defending the practice which was to be found, not only in Iran, but in neighboring Sunni countries, of prostration before the monarch. The entirety of the religious hierarchy was headed by a certain official known as the *sadr al-mamalik* whose function it was to distribute patronage of the state and to ensure the obedience and loyalty of the class of *ulama* as a whole.

There were, however, dissident voices. At the very height of Safavid power during the reign of Shah Abbas (1587-1629), we find the *ulama* for the first time within the context of Iran, enunciating the essential political theory of the Shi'a, of the dubious legitimacy of monarchy and existing government. One of the contemporaries of Shah Abbas, Mulla Ahmad Ardabili, encountered Shah Abbas on a certain occasion and reminded him that his monarchy, his power, was held not by divine right, nor as a result of any particular fitness on his part, but rather as something that was a trust on behalf of the Imam and that if the trust were violated, and the hint was there that the trust was being violated, then the *ulama* had the right to remove the trust from the king. This, as far as I know, is one of the earliest recorded instances of the disputation of the legitimacy of the royal power in Shi'i Iran. In addition, the French traveller Chardin, who spent several years in Iran during the mid-seventeenth century, reports having heard some religious scholars advance the claim that a properly qualified *mujtahid* — a term to be explained below — should rule, not a king of questionable morals and piety.

The increased assertiveness this may be taken to reflect shows itself above all in the career of Mulla Muhammad Baqir Majlisi, one of the most prolific and influential scholars of the whole Safavid period. It is true that he espoused a certain kind of legitimacy for the monarchy, which drew on the traditional Iranian ideal of the justice-dispensing king, but in so doing he envisaged the monarch as essentially an executive officer, to be supervised by the religious scholars in the fulfillment of his duties. For he exercised a dominating influence himself over the Safavid state during the closing years of the seventeenth century. It is true that the nature and consequences of that influence have sometimes been negatively evaluated, but the important fact to be retained from a broad historical perspective is the rise of a powerful Shi'i scholar to a position of dominance. Majlisi might serve as a point of departure for the rewriting of Iranian history suggested above.

With the effective end of the Safavid dynasty in 1722 a period of anarchy began in Iran. At one point within the eighteenth century we find no fewer than thirteen different contestants for the throne doing battle with each other. This disintegration of the political authority accelerated the process of divorce between the religious institution and the monarchy. We can say that in the absence of an effective centralized monarchy throughout the eighteenth century the *ulama* often were able, in a practical fashion, quite apart from theoretical developments that I shall discuss later, to assume the role of local governors, arbitrators of disputes, executors of law, and so forth. By the end of the eighteenth century, the new dynasty had emerged that was able gradually to impose its rule on the entirety of Iran -- the Qajar dynasty. However, the Qajars (1779-1924) were in no position to continue the same relationship with the *ulama* that the Safavids had enjoyed at the beginning of their powers. On the very eve of the rise of the Qajar dynasty we find taking place among the religious class an important debate on a seemingly technical matter, which had the greatest of political consequences as well. This debate took place between the two schools known as the Usuli and the Akhbari. This debate was on a matter that appeared to be technical, relating to the details of Islamic jurisprudence.

To summarize briefly the positions of the two schools, the Akhbaris, as their name indicates, maintain that in the absence of the Imam it was not permissible for a religious scholar to engage in the use of his reason to enact a certain judgement, to apply the principles of the law to a specific problem or situation. What had to be done was always to have recourse to *hadith*; hence the word *akhbari*, and on the basis of the sifting of those *hadith* to arrive at a conclusion, with respect to a particular problem. In short, we can say that the Akhbaris held that every *alim* should be above all a scholar of *hadith* and that he had little legitimate competence beyond that. In other words, they tended totally to an abolition of the whole discipline of legal methodology known as *usul al-fiqh*. The Usulis, by contrast, said that this was not the case and even in the absence of the Imam it was permissible to engage in independent reasoning with respect to legal questions, of course on the basis of the sources of law as defined by the Shi'a. Hence the designation given to them, Usuli. They were those who believed there were a certain number of principles of law, sources of law, that could be applied and interpreted through the use of the individual reasoning of the qualified scholar. The qualified scholar in question is the *mujtahid*, that is literally he who, in a technically defined fashion, exercises his reasoning powers on the basis of the principles of law to arrive at a ruling concerning a given problem. There is some confusion in that the word *mujtahid* has a particular application in Sunni Islam to the founders of the four *madhhabs*. Its usage in Shi'ism does not have such a wide connotation. It is not a question of each individual putting forward a new *madhhab*, a complete system of legal principles and rulings. It is a question of a more limited kind of independent reasoning.

The *mujtahid* is not merely a legal authority, one who can give an expression of opinion in this fashion concerning a problem of Islamic law; he is also a person whose views, under certain circumstances, must be followed. The Usulis believe that in the absence of the Imam, the entirety of the community is divided into those who are either *mujtahids* or who are not *mujtahids*. If they are not *mujtahids*, that is if they do not have the necessary power of comprehension of the law and independent reasoning to attain that state, they must of necessity follow the guidance of one who is, and this following of guidance is known as *taqlid*. The common connotation of the word is *imitation*, but it has a technical meaning of following the guidance of a qualified religious scholar in the specific ordinances of law.

Given the fact that Islamic law in its scope knows of no distinction between the secular and the religious, given the fact that the affairs of state and the economy and society all fall within the scope of the Islamic law, it follows that the guidance dispensed by the *mujtahid* may have significant political consequences. Hence it is that every Shi'i Muslim who is not himself a *mujtahid* is bound to follow a *mujtahid* as his *marja'-i taqlid*, i.e., source of authority to whom he implicity pledges obedience by his choice.

Were it not for the triumph of the Usuli position in the eighteenth century on the eve of the rise of Qajars, there would have been no *mujtahids*, or if there had been, their positions would have been contested. The religious scholars in general would have found themselves condemned to an extremely marginal position, to the sifting of the *ahadith*, the narrations and traditions of the Prophet and the Imams (on whom be peace), with little ability to provide living and continuous guidance for the affairs of society and politics at large. One may say that the Revolution in Iran, at least the particular shape that it has taken, the form of leadership that it has enjoyed and continues to enjoy, would also have been unthinkable without this triumph of the Usuli position in this apparently technical dispute in the eighteenth century.

To come now to the Qajar period, given this triumph of the Usuli position and the emergence of a strong class of *mujtahids*, convinced of their authority not merely as the interpreters of tradition but as the executors of tradition and law, the Qajars found their position disputed from the beginning. First, this disputation of the authority of the Qajar monarchs took place sporadically with respect to certain particular issues or events. Throughout the early part of the nineteenth century we find a number of provincial governors being expelled from the cities they were supposed to rule by the people of those cities who had been empowered, or even instructed, to do so by the local *mujtahid*. An early example of the opposition of the *ulama* or the *mujtahids* to the royal power is to be seen in 1826 when Muslims inhabiting territories that had been captured from Iran in the first Russo-Iranian war were subject to religious persecution at the hands of the Russians. The *ulama* then delivered a judgment to the effect that it was the duty of Iran to go to war against Russia. The monarch of the day initially showed considerable reluctance; whereupon, according to a British diplomatic dispatch of the time, the most influential of the *mujtahids* of the day was reported to have said that "unless this present Shah does our bidding and obeys our *fatva*, we shall remove him and put another dog in his place."

Throughout the century the antagonism between the *ulama* and the monarchy became more and more intense. In part this was because of the logical implications of the political theory of the Shi'a, amplified by the emergence of the Usuli *madhhab*. Another important factor was the growing alliance between the Iranian monarchy and foreign powers. Now the monarchy was seen not merely to be holding a power of dubious legitimacy, not merely to be flouting the law of Islam, to be an instrument of tyranny and injustice; it was seen to be the agent for increasing foreign encroachment upon Iran and exploitation of its resources. It is hardly surprising therefore that we see the first mass movement of modern Iranian history directed against foreign hegemony in Iran led by the Shi'i *ulama*. In 1892 the production and marketing of tobacco within Iran and outside had been given to a British monopoly. The leading *mujtahid* of the day, Mirza Hasan Shirazi, gave a *fatva* to the effect that for as long as tobacco was cultivated and marketed by this monopoly it was forbidden to be consumed. Such was the effect of this *fatva* that even the women in the royal household refrained from the use of tobacco. This movement in 1892 was followed just over a decade later by the movement in Iranian history known as the Constitutional Revolution, which dates approximately from 1905 until 1911.

In the Constitutional Revolution the *ulama* continued to play an extremely important role, influencing its whole course in a member of ways. It is of course true that constitutionalism, even the word itself or the word that it is intended to translate, is of European origin and it may be asked how could it be that the *ulama*, whether in Iran or any other Islamic country, could adopt a course, a method of political reform that is obviously foreign in its ultimate origins. The answer that can be given, at least in the case of Iran, is fairly clear. It was held by many Shi'i *ulama* of the day that a totally legitimate authority was, in the nature of things, impossible given the continuing occultation or absence of the Imam from the world. It was held that all that could be done in his absence was to limit the inevitable illegitimacy of existing rule. Therefore a monarchical power that was limited by the existence of a constitution, by the election of an assembly of representatives, was preferable to one that was absolute and arbitrary in its exercise of power. Hence the idea of constitutionalism, which had been introduced into Iran by certain western educated elements, was given a particular application and content by the *ulama*. They saw in it a means of limiting the royal power and lessening the illegitimacy that was almost inevitable in their view in the whole institution of the state. It is not possible or even necessary to relate to you the events of the Iranian Constitutional Revolution. Enough to say that the major Iranian historian of the Revolution, Ahmad Kasravi, has seen in the agreement concluded in November 1905 by the two major *mujtahids* of Tehran, Sayyid Muhammad Bihbihani and Sayyid Muhammad Tabatabai, the starting point of the Revolution. Throughout the Revolution the major directives came from the *ulama*.[1]

The Iranian Constitutional Revolution was in large part frustrated by the resistance of the monarchy, powerfully supported and encouraged by foreign powers. We may say that had it not been for the continued interference in Iranian affairs first by Russia, then by Great Britain, and most recently by the United States and Israel, Iran today, instead of looking back on a quarter century of struggle and a year of revolution in which at least fifty thousand people were slaughtered, might will have been able to look back on more than half a century of constitutional and parliamentary rule. As it was, first the Russians, then the British, and recently the Americans frustrated aspirations for popular government in Iran. Here also we cannot go into detail. Time does not permit it. The Russians dominated in much of the period from 1908, until the First World War, by the end of which the British had appeared in force on the scene — in such force that they had

---

[1] It should, of course, be borne in mind that by no means all the *ulama* favored the constitutional movement, and that not all those who did were consistent in their support (see the discussion of Shaikh Fazlullah Nuri below). Those who were opposed or came to change their minds found objectionable some of the secularizing premises of the constitution. It should also be noted that, despite the predominance of ulama in its early stages, the Constitutional Revolution represented a coalition of different ideological forces, by contrast with the Islamic Revolution, where the participation of secular or leftist forces was strictly marginal. Precisely this difference helps to explain the ultimate failure of the former and the success of the latter.

no visible competitor — and brought about a change of dynasty from the Qajar to the Pahlavi dynasty, now happily defunct. With the Pahlavi dynasty a new period was inaugurated in the history of Iran, a new and particularly somber period in which the traditional monarchy is transformed into a modern dictatorship.

It was often said in the United States and probably elsewhere that the Iranian Revolution was motivated by hostility to this glorious phenomenon known as "modernization." In so far as the word "modernization" has had any meaning in the Iranian context, what was modernized by the Pahlavi dynasty was the apparatus of repression. At least the Qajar dynasty and the others before it were limited in their ability to enact their will by the traditional inefficiency of Middle Eastern monarchies; but by contrast the Pahlavi dynasty, although it paid lip service to Iranian tradition, and thanks to British aid and encouragement laid hold of the crown of Iran, in effect ruled as dictators of a modern, European, totalitarian kind. It followed that under this kind of regime the constitutional ideal to which the *ulama* from a particular point of view had subscribed was thoroughly repressed and defeated. We find therefore in the period of Reza Khan, the first member of this two-man dynasty, the coming into being of a rubber stamp parliamentary assembly. That continued effectively to be the case until the overthrow of the monarchy, with the partial exception of a few years immediately after the Second World War. Among the few individuals to resist the imposition of the Pahlavi dictatorship in an open fashion was one of the *ulama*, Sayyid Hasan Mudarris. He spoke up in the Majlis against the measures of Reza Khan and went into exile where after an interval he was murdered by agents of Reza Khan.

Another characteristic of the period, apart from the suppression of constitutionalism, is the imitation of the measures taken in neighboring Turkey by Mustafa Kamal. An attempt was made to cultivate an ethnic nationalism with strong overtones of hatred against the Arabs, rejection of the Islamic heritage, glorification of the pre-Islamic past, the purging of the Persian language of Arabic loan words, and so on. For a variety of reasons the measures taken by Reza Khan in Iran were less effective than those that had taken place in Turkey partly because imitation is always less successful than the original and partly because westernization and secularization had a far longer prehistory in Turkey and the Ottoman State than in Iran. In any event, this officially sponsored nationalist ideology continued to dominate at least the surface of Iranian life for many years, so much so that a large number of western observers were happy to write off Iran as a constituent part of the Islamic world and were given to repeating the remarks made by Iranian officialdom, "Yes, we are Muslims, but remember we are not Arabs," as if there were some kind of tension between these two entities. In fact the continuing and effective loyalty of the great mass of the Iranian people to Islam, with all of the alignments that that implies, never ceased. It was simply that the open manifestation of it became difficult if not impossible for many years under the rule of the two successive Pahlavi dictators.

In 1941 the reign of the first Pahlavi monarch came to an end. The same people — the British — who had installed him first deposed and them removed him from the country. On this occasion they were aided by the Americans and the Russians. As the second Shah indicated in his own memoirs, in a very interesting sentence, "It was deemed appropriate by the Allies that I should succeed my father." So this then young man who was put on the throne in 1941 commenced his rule of exploitation and repression in the service of his foreign masters. The change of ruler in itself resulted, however in a temporary relaxation of the full rigor of Pahlavi rule. In the first decade of the reign of the now deposed Shah we see a resurgence of Islamically oriented elements in the political life of the country. The ideal pursued is for the most part constitutionalism, and politically active *ulama* of the time, such as Ayatullah Kashani, in the numerous speeches he made within the Iranian parliament and outside, would always refer to two sources of authority — on the one hand the Qur'an, and on the other hand the Iranian Constitution. In the name of both the Constitution and the Qur'an he would call for the nationalization of the Iranian oil industry, in order to bring to an end British domination of

Iran, and he would call, too, for an effective limitation on the royal power. Outside of the Majlis, there was a large number of Islamic elements at work in this period. There were, for example, the Fidayan-e Islam. They produced a blueprint for an Islamic state in Iran, and did not hesitate to assassinate those they identified as agents of the British and therefore as enemies of Islam, such as Prime Minister Razmara. But the dominant political personality of this first decade of the prewar period was not a member of the religious class. He was a secular nationalist politician, the late Dr. Mohammad Musaddiq, who nonetheless enjoyed the support of many in the religious classes. Partly because of the ideological confusions of the period, that support was by no means total.

We know now in full detail what happened to Dr. Musaddiq and the nationalist regime he headed. It was the direct intervention of the United States in the form of the CIA coup of August 1953 that brought about the overthrow of Dr. Musaddiq and the return of the Shah from the exile into which he had fled.

The return of the Shah in 1953 inaugurated the intense period of a quarter of a century of unprecedented massacre and repression and the intensive exploitation of the resources of the Iranian people by the imperialism of the East and West, the western camp now being headed by the United States rather than Britain. In that period, of course, a large number of ideological forces came into being to combat the dictatorship of the Shah and his subservience to foreign powers. But from the beginning, immediately after the coup of 1953, we see religious elements playing an important part. We can mention what was called the National Resistance Movement that came into being very soon after the return of the Shah from exile. Although there is no overtly religious component in the designation of this organization, it was succeeded somewhat later by a movement called the Movement of God-Fearing Socialists. It should be said that at this time socialism in Iran, or at least a certain variety of socialism, enjoyed a certain vogue because of the popularity of the slogan of "Islamic socialism" in the Arab world. This is not the time to go into the suitability or otherwise of this term. I mention it in passing.

Then we had in 1962 the emergence to public and political prominence for the first time of the present leader of the Iranian people, Ayatullah Ruhullah Khomeini. About his immediate background I will speak in much greater detail at my next lecture. To place him for the moment in the historical perspective I have attempted to sketch for you this morning, we can say that he is in many ways the culmination of a long tradition that begins with the first hesitant disputation of the legitimacy of the monarchy. That goes on in the Qajar period to openly contest the authority of the monarchy in a certain number of specific incidents. It proceeds to the attempt to limit the power of the monarchy through a constitution, and then sees that the whole formality of legalism, constitutionalism of itself, is not adequate and that nothing short of revolution and the complete overthrow of the existing order is acceptable. It is part of the greatness of Imam Khomeini to have given a leadership and direction to the Islamic Revolution that is totally without parallel in the contemporary Islamic world. Without in any way diminishing or underestimating the importance of his personal contribution, one should bear in mind that he has behind him a long tradition upon which he draws, a tradition of self-assertion by the *ulama* as the directive force in society, a tradition of opposition to rule precisely in the name of Shi'i Islam, a tradition of ever growing militancy and constant readiness to self-sacrifice.

These are the main points I wanted to mention today. There has inevitably been much omission and oversimplification, names left out, and so forth. Perhaps I can partially make up for that in the second segment of our meeting today.

Discussion

Question: You have attributed the preservation of the monarchy, even though it was viewed as an illegitimate institution, to the influence of external forces. To what extent is the inability to develop alternative institutions to the monarchy a reflection of an inadequate political theory or the absence of the development of an adequate political formulation within Muslim thinking in the last few centuries? Will there always be this tension between state authority and the Ayatullah within the Shi'i tradition and what is there to prevent this tension being removed to allow for the development of a new constitution?

HA: As to the persistence of the monarchy in Iran, to put it more precisely I should have said that the monarchy was able to defy and subvert the constitution in part because of the support of foreign powers. The religious leaders earlier in the century were willing to support the continued existence of the monarchy on the condition that the constitution was observed, which was rarely if ever the case. There was gradual evolution in the conclusions drawn from the political situation. The conclusion was first drawn that the illegitimacy inherent in any state in the absence of the Imam, at the time of the Constitutional Revolution, might be reduced, if not abolished, through the institution of the constitution.[2] When the constitutional experiment failed, gradually realization dawned that the institution of monarchy should be abolished.

Moreover, one of the important contributions of Imam Khomeini that I should mention is that he takes issue with the whole idea of the inevitable suspension of Islamic government during the absence of the Imam. In a series of lectures that he gave under the title "Islamic Government," originally given largely to an audience of *ulama* and students of religious sciences, he says that because the Imam is absent does this mean that the *shari'a*

---

[2] This was the view above all of Mirza Muhammad Husayn Na'ini, expounded in his book *Tanbih al-Umma wa Tanzih al-Milla.*

should no longer be enforced? Obviously not. If the *shari'a* is to be enforced, there must be those who enforce the *shari'a*. In other words, there must be a political authority that is firmly based upon the authority of the *shari'a*.

As for a tension between the Ayatullah (i.e., Imam Khomeini) and the secular authorities, probably you are alluding to the so-called rift between Imam Khomeini and Mehdi Bazargan — a charge played up greatly in the western press as if there was some fundamental antagonism between the two men, which is not the case. Bazargan has the unusual quality, although in some cases it is not always an advantage, of speaking his mind in a very precise and frank fashion, whoever or whatever the audience may be. Therefore he comments in the frankest possible way upon any problems that come up in his relations with Imam Khomeini in the revolutionary situation. This is not a question of a fundamental antagonism between the two men on a personal or institutional level. There is no question of a continuation in the postrevolutionary period of attitudes that are somehow irreconcilable.[3]

Dr Kalim Siddiqui: There appears to have been a lag in the development of Muslim political thought over this period. The lag has been taken up by Imam Khomeini. In other words, the political thought was lagging behind the actual situation.

HA: I think it is true to say that. It is justifiable to say that there was a lack of a fully articulated political theory and it was largely stimulated by the evolution of circumstances in Iran. After the constitutional experiment essentially failed and after the massive repression took place under the auspices of the United States and Israel,

---

[3] This assessment of the relationship between the late Bazargan and the Imam is undeniably erroneous, although the Western media did exaggerate the degree to which differences between the two men and the mentalities they represented were able to threaten the revolution. My contrasting underestimation preceded my own first visit to Iran after the revolution, in December 1979, when in conversation with me Bazargan expressed attitudes frankly hostile to the ulama. More significantly, statements by the Imam were subsequently published to the effect that the appointment of Bazargan had been a mistake.

people were led inevitably to have new thoughts on the matter and to take up more uncompromising, more far-reaching positions than had been the case in the past.

Question: May I raise the same question? It refers to the problem of illegitimacy of any government in the absence of the Imam. I find it difficult to trace a point where in the existence of the Imam — there were twelve Imams who have existed over two centuries — there has ever been an attempt to displace the existing monarchy. No Imam, to my knowledge, has ever taken up arms against the rulers who are, ipso facto, considered illegitimate.

HA: There are two contradictory conclusions that may be drawn from the illegitimacy of existing power. One tends in the direction of quietism and the other in the direction of open manifestation. One important doctrine of Shi'ism which operated in the direction of quietism was *taqiya*, the preservation of the community through its virtual self-effacement in a political sense. After the disappearance of the Imam both options were open, that of quietism or revolutionary action. Progressively under the impact of particular circumstances the second course came to be chosen.

Comment: As a result of this policy of isolating Iran from the Arab world and also as a result of degeneration of scholarship in the Muslim and Arab world and the Sunni world, the Sunnis know very little about the Shi'i, so much so that the term *Ayatullah*, when it became well known at the end of last year and the beginning of this year, was completely unknown. It would be useful for many of us, who are Sunnis, to hear something from you about this office and whether there is a structure, a hierarchy, through which the authority passes.

HA: The term Ayatullah is literally translated as "a sign of God" — a person who, through his spiritual and learned attainments, is a manifestation of certain qualities that ultimately draw upon divine perfection. It is a title given by popular usage; in other words, it does not denote a function, like *mujtahid*. It is a title conferred by popular usage on someone who has emerged as one of the major *mujtahids*. We cannot speak of a hierarchy within the Shi'a other than the simple hierarchy of *mujtahid* and *muqallid*. Essentially the Shi'i community is composed of *mujtahids* and *muqallids*. Among the *mujtahids* there are those who have the greatest authority and degree of learning. It sometimes happens that among the *mujtahids* a certain individual will emerge as the sole *marja'-i taqlid*. In other words, the personal attainments of that person are such that he will overshadow all of the *mujtahids* and everyone will exercise *taqlid* in respect of him.

Comment: How many *maraji'-i taqlid* are there? I read that there are six Ayatullahs in Iran.

HA: No, there are many more than that. The title has become a little over generously used recently. There are probably about four or five *maraji'-i taqlid*[4] of whom Imam Khomeini is the most important.

Imam Khomeini in a political sense is the *marja'-i taqlid* of people who in nonpolitical matters follow the guidance of other *mujtahids*. You find people who are in a narrow sense the followers of Ayatullah Shari'atmadari but who politically follow Imam Khomeini.[5] His authority has gone far beyond the bounds of what is implied in this whole doctrine of *taqlid*, although that is the technical basis for it. He exercises a far wider authority.

Dr Kalim Siddiqui: These *marji'-i taqlid* are not elected?

HA: Not in a formal sense. Since there is no machinery, no elective machinery, no machinery of appointment, it is not as though

---

[4] *Maraji'-i taqlid* is the plural of *marja'-i taqlid*.

[5] This combination of loyalties was still in place at the time of my first visit to revolutionary Iran in December 1979, but was already beginning to decline as a result of anarchic activities by the followers of Shari'atmadari, grouped in the Hizb-i Khalq-i Musalman, in Tabriz and elsewhere.

someone puts himself up for the office. It is simply that one attains the technical qualification of *mujtahid*, and then through the piety and learning he demonstrates he gathers a certain following. His influence will be mediated to his following by, if you like, the second-ranking members of the *ulama*. Here is where you can speak of a network in Iran. I do not like the word "hierarchy," but one can speak of a network.

When I was in Paris with Imam Khomeini at the end of last year, it was interesting to see how the various proclamations and instructions of Imam Khomeini were conveyed. A telephone call was made from Paris to a number of provincial cities in Iran. Every individual seated at his telephone in each of those cities would have a tape recorder ready. The message would be recorded, transcribed, and given into the hands of the local *ulama* for distribution within that city. In turn, the students of those *ulama* would take it out into the villages. This is one of the things I should have spoken of but did not get the chance to. The work of Imam Khomeini was preceded in an organizational sense and made possible by the work of Ayatullah Burujirdi. He was politically inactive; when there was the struggle for nationalizing the oil industry, when there was the American coup d'etat against Dr. Mussadeq, he remained silent. That silence earned him the reproaches of many people. But one important achievement that is to his credit is the reorganization of what is called Hauza-yi Ilmiya, the teaching institution in Qum. He established a network for the dissemination of religious knowledge throughout Iran as well as the collection of *zakat* and *khums*. The same network established by him was used later by Imam Khomeini and other leaders.

Comment: The world press is rather contradictory. Some people say we cannot shut our eyes to the prosperity and achievement brought about by the Shah of Iran, for example, in education, industry, and even in the number of doctors. There are more doctors in Iran than in Pakistan or other countries. This was done in the reign of the king himself. Second, this killing that continues by Imam Khomeini — it is judicial or unjudicial assassination. What do you call it? There is a long list of killings. In spite of the world press (which says that this should be stopped in the interests of Iran because there should be a reconciliation between the people working under the regime of the Shah and others because the target is almost achieved), the king is expelled from the soil. The killing is almost meaningless. There should be complete reconciliation and unity to bring about cooperation in Islamic structure.

HA: Since this question has been raised, I think that I should answer it. I have to say that I think it is unfortunate that a Muslim should raise this kind of question and put forward these ideas. You speak of a continuation of the killings. If you equate the cold-blooded slaughter of fifty thousand people in a single year — I am not speaking of the entire career of the Shah - with the execution of three hundred murderers by the Islamic revolutionary regime in Iran, you must have a strange conception of justice in general and Islamic justice in particular. It is not a question of judicial assassination — I am not quite sure what that means — surely in Islam a murderer is accountable for his crimes and someone who is guilty of multiple murder should also be accountable. You speak about unity. Unity between whom and on what basis? There can be no unity between on the one hand the people who have offered thousands of sacrifices and martyrs, whose blood is hardly yet dry on the streets of Iran, and on the other hand those who for the United States, the Soviet Union, Britain, Israel, and other centers of corruption and intrigue around the world have been continually slaughtering and murdering their own fellow countrymen. How can there be unity between them? On the contrary, the number of people executed in Iran since the Revolution has been extremely small and extremely restrained. In the United States the Zionist hypocrites who control the media talk about a bloodbath in Iran. Where were these people when on a single day in Iran, September 8, 1978, some four thousand people were shot down? Now you want to have forgiveness and reconciliation. No. These butchers should be put to death. Those who have fled to other countries, these thieves, embezzlers, these drug merchants, if they be in Britain or anywhere else, as the Chief of the Revolutionary Council said, they deserve to be brought to justice.

Question: As we know, the western press and the media are controlled by Zionists, imperialists, and intriguers. Justice has to be seen to be done and to be carried out as regards the perpetrators of injustices and the western people who have been committing murders against the people of Iran. Will we be cowed by the western media and the intriguers as regards the carrying out of justice in Iran?

HA: One thing we should remember as Muslims is that we have our own form of judicial procedure in Islam. The Iranian people did not suffer the sacrifices that they did to have a replica, a pale imitation of some western form of government, whether a judicial system, political organization, or anything else. For us as Muslims the only relevant question is whether the trials and executions that have taken place in Iran are in conformity with Islamic practice and standards. Very clearly they are. Every individual who has been accused and brought before a court in Iran has had the chance of calling witnesses for and against. Those who have a direct interest in the case have been permitted to attend, representatives of the foreign press have attended certain of the trials, although not all of them. We hear of "hasty justice" from some segments of the western press. What is meant by this? In Islam if a judgement is given that is fully supported by the evidence, there is no logical or human reason to delay the execution of that judgement. It is more merciful.

Question: We have discussed the tradition and leadership of the Iranian movement and the Revolution, which is the outstanding event in the Muslim world. Would you consider such background developments to be a prerequisite or otherwise for the Islamic Revolution?

HA: You are anticipating something that forms the topic of a later lecture. In my last lecture to you I want to consider this question of the applicability of the Iranian model to other Muslim countries. To give a partial and preliminary answer, the emergence of an *ulama* class in the form we have seen in Iran is not a prerequisite for the success of the Islamic movement in other parts of the Islamic world because this would in effect mean that they all accept Shi'ism, which of course they are free to do, but I do not think we can say that this in itself is a prerequisite. There are other lessons to be drawn from the Iranian experience that are to be designated as prerequisites. On the one hand there is the clear identification of the existing order as being totally opposed to Islam; the refusal of any cooperation with it or absorption into it; the total and realistic and serious opposition that brings with it a readiness to sacrifice; a shunning of the various forms of pseudo-Islamic activities, such as attending conferences in Saudi Arabia, and so forth. Imam Khomeini has never attended a single conference sponsored by the Saudi regime and yet we see him today not merely the de facto ruler of Iran, but the source of inspiration to millions of Muslims throughout the world. These and other lessons of the Iranian Revolution I would like to draw on later.

Question: The question of the struggle of the Iranian *ulama* seems to be one of turning back to the role of religious counselors or advisers during the postrevolutionary period. How far is this true? The *ulama* played the role of religious counselors, but now Khomeini has not put these men as secretaries of state or as prime minister.

HA: I understand the reason for your question, but I think it implies a number of things that are not true. You talk about a secretary of state. The minister of foreign affairs in Iran is by no means a secularist.[6] I am sure you would agree that for a Muslim to avoid

---

6 The Minister of Foreign Affairs at the time was Ibrahim Yazdi, of whom it is fair to say that in the course of time he has indeed evolved into being a secularist, at least in the sense of rejecting *vilayat-i faqih*.

being a secularist it is not necessary for him to wear a turban. The government is made up of people who are fully committed to Islam. I do not think that Imam Khomeini has withdrawn from a prominent, indeed, a leading role in Iran. There is a duality of authority that we now see in Iran. The Revolutionary Council is composed mainly, if not exclusively, of religious authorities. The provisional revolutionary government is made up of people who have administrative experience that, for obvious reasons, members of the religious class lack. On the other hand, the wise decision was made by Imam Khomeini not to put religious leaders in a position of obvious prominence so as to avoid the accusation that an Islamic state means rule by the *ulama*, which obviously it does not. There is this temporary arrangement, which will come to an end once the constitution has been ratified and, on the basis of the constitution, elections have been held. Then the government that emerges on the basis of elections may be composed exclusively of non-*ulama* elements. It might be composed exclusively of *ulama* elements or more likely a mixture of the two. There is a party called the Party for the Islamic Republic, the governing body of which, composed of six individuals, belongs exclusively to the *ulama*. There is a great likelihood that when the elections take place, it will win an absolute majority.

Dr Kalim Siddiqui: Can I take you up on this? I detected a number of contradictions. One of them is the existence of administrative experience among a group of people. Earlier you said that there should be no compromise with the existing system. Now you are saying that you want to rely in the early period of the Revolution on experience gained in the past. How do you gain experience from that political system and how is the political experience of that period relevant to this period? My other question is that it seems that you are now saying that there will be elections in which a political party called the Party for the Islamic Republic will fight for election. This assumes that there would be another party or could be, technically, another party opposing that party, which does not want an Islamic republic. In that event you are relying on the attainment of a majority. When was an election last held in a Shi'i political system? What is the origin of elections in the political system of the Islamic republic? In all of this you seem to be dipping your hands back into the foreigners' basket for intellectual and technical tools.

HA: As to the first question about the acquisition of experience by members of the present provisional government, they acquired their experience in the period of Dr. Musaddiq, which makes it reasonably creditable. Prime Minister Bazargan managed the Iranian oil industry immediately after its nationalization. Others in the present cabinet have had experience not in the government as such but rather in the spheres of academia, or in some cases in technical enterprises that were independent of the state in the period of the Shah. It is not a question of taking on people who have acquired experience of political administration under the regime of the Shah. Moreover, they are being deployed at the moment not in the formulation of policy but in its execution. I agree that it is not entirely satisfactory that there should be this duality of authority. One must remember that this is an interim and transitional situation in which contradictions are bound to exist and which, we hope, will be resolved.

Turning now to the second question about elections and the place of them in Shi'ism. There is no question of elections when it comes to the Imam from the Ahl al-Bayt who is divinely appointed. However, whether one be Shi'i or Sunni, there is the simple factor of the Qur'anic injunction for consultation. An election is nothing more than a mechanism for the implementation of this general Qur'anic principle of consultation. Another point that is of importance and significance about the Islamic Revolution is that it feels secure enough of itself, sufficiently self-assured, to permit the expression of dissenting points of view. It is surely a far more effective way of combating the potential danger represented by Marxism to permit the free organization of Marxist political parties and then in the electoral process to demonstrate their impotence than it is to jump upon them and put their members in jail, as if Muslims had something to be scared of. This anticommunist bogey that is waved in various parts of the Muslim world to frighten people into silence should be brought into the open and shown for what it is, as something totally weak.

Moreover, there is the simple question that we cannot have an Islamic state based upon coercion. To permit freedom of expression, even in opposition to the principle of an Islamic Republic, seems politically wise and in accordance with the fundamental injunctions of Islam itself.[7]

Question: In the light of the Shi'i concept of political authority, if this concept was to be extended from a particular country, say that of Iran, who will make that political authority? Will it be a central authority? If it is a central authority, who will make it and will there be agreements upon it? If that is not the case, will it be independent local authorities and do you see any political differences of opinion?

HA: We have to admit that there is no single uniquely valid system of political authority. There are certain general principles that may apply in different fashions according to certain particular circumstances. Whether the forms that are in the process of emerging in Iran will be applicable without modification to other countries, it is a question that remains open. Your questions pertain to a number of matters that belong to later lectures. One important factor about the Iranian Revolution that makes it a real revolution and not a coup d'etat, is that the people before the Revolution to some degree evolved their own organs of government and administration. This took place before the final triumph of the Revolution. The removal of Shapur Bakhtiar was a formality because an alternative government had come into being and,

---

[7] This generous interpretation of the "freedom of expression" permitted by Islam now strikes me as questionable. In any event, it is plain enough that active opposition to the fundamental principles of the Islamic Republic is not tolerated in Iran.

moreover, this had happened while Imam Khomeini was still in exile.

There is in Iran at the moment a large dispersal of authority, a decentralization. This is something valuable from which every Muslim can learn. Frequently in other Islamic movements, whether in the Arab world, Pakistan, or elsewhere, when they speak of an Islamic state the idea is of setting up a strong central authority geared to realizing the goals of Islam and then telling the people how to implement these goals. What has happened in Iran is the opposite, namely that there has emerged in every village throughout the country a local organ of self-government and authority that functions with the mosque as its center, with the local *ulama* as its leaders who effectively conduct the day-to-day business of government.

The new draft constitution, interestingly enough, provides for the perpetuation of this feature. The field is definitely open for experimentation. One of the valuable things that has happened in Iran is that for the first time, not on the basis of some theoretical concepts drawn up by so-called Islamic research academies, but on the basis of the true and genuine revolutionary participation by the whole people, a viable model of government has come into being. Whether other Muslim countries follow this model is another question. The important thing about what is happening in Iran is that it has been a mass movement that has evolved its own form of self-government. It has not been a question of theory. Other movements elsewhere have been strong on theory and have spent lots of conference time debating this, generally abroad in America and Europe. But they have been weak in practice. You can reproach the Iranian movement with late development of a theory, but you cannot reproach it with lack of practice. Lack of theory is the less essential factor.

Dr. Kalim Siddiqui: It seems to me that in your lecture you were saying that over three hundred years in Iran there developed Shi'i intellectual thought and there was a process of development of thought in Iran that has led to this Revolution. You rightly linked

Imam Khomeini with all the major figures who articulated Shi'i thought or Islamic thought in Iran leading up to this Revolution. Now you appear to be saying that there was no need for the intellectual basis of the Revolution.

HA: No, I am not saying that. No one disputes the necessity of intellectual pursuit, but an intellectual pursuit that is carried on in isolation or at the expense of actual practice and actual involvement in the day-to-day problems of Muslims, the Muslim masses, is something else. That is something totally useless.

Question: The Islamic Revolution in Iran has brought about a change in the role of leadership in the Islamic system as compared to other systems. Could you briefly comment on how the leadership role differs in different systems?

HA: This is a generalized question. Rather than attempt a comparison, I would say that Imam Khomeini has emerged as the leader of the Iranian people. I do not like this word *leader* because it carries a certain kind of connotation with it. That is, it does so in English, where we are obliged to make compromises. He has emerged, for want of a better word, as the leader of the Iranian people. Here again, I may be sounding anti-intellectual, but it is not because of a question of theory. All this theory I have elaborated has been of importance, but it is not primarily a question of what Imam Khomeini has done and is doing; it is a question of what the man is. Anyone who has come into the presence of Imam Khomeini has realized that this man is a kind of embodiment of the human ideal. It is by exercising this combination of moral, intellectual, political, and spiritual ability that he has come to have this tremendous role in Iran. He has gone far beyond the traditional bounds of authority of the *marja'-i taqlid*. He has become a symbol, an incorporation of the whole Iranian Muslim concept of self-identity. If Muslims look at him, non-Iranian Muslims, they will see in him a precious example of the human ideal of Islam also.

This is a man who today can have a demonstration of millions of people on the streets in Iran in a few minutes. Yet when you see him in his place of work and his residence, he is sitting on the floor with a little lectern in front of him. That is the entirety of his office equipment. Yet you can go to so-called Muslim leaders — this is the relevant comparison — and see them in their comfortably appointed offices. I recall visiting an apartment in Ankara belonging to a prominent leader of a party that with some justice calls itself an Islamic party. This was an apartment overstuffed with all kinds of souvenirs of trips to western Europe, with pseudo-French furniture and gold-plated telephones. Yet this was one of the people who claimed to represent Islam. I am not saying that Imam Khomeini is totally unique in his personal way of life. There have been others and there are others in the Islamic world who have at least approached the same ideal. But if you are speaking in general about the qualities of leadership, it is not a question of a particular theory of leadership or a certain organization or network; it is to do with the peculiarity of this man, the spiritual and moral dimension that must be there. With Imam Khomeini obviously and overwhelmingly it is there. I read an interesting article by a Turkish secularist newspaperman who, before the Iranian Revolution, like many other writers in the Turkish daily press, had written all kinds of nonsense about Imam Khomeini. This writer had gone to see Imam Khomeini. It was interesting. He said he went in the presence of Imam Khomeini with a whole list of idiotic questions, such as, "What about women?," "Are you going to dismantle the factories?," and that kind of junk. Instead of putting forward this series of questions, he found himself reduced to complete silence and a great sense of shame and embarrassment. In the end the only question he could ask Imam Khomeini was for some guidance in his personal life. Whereupon he was advised to study Islam and begin making his prayers, and so on.

Anyone who has the honor of seeing Imam Khomeini has the same story. It is what the man is. All too often in this pseudointellectualism the Muslims waste their time and energy. You totally lose sight of the end. You sit around arguing about words. You lose sight of those spiritual and moral qualities. It is not a matter of sentimentalism or spiritualism. This is a demonstrable reality. How else can we explain the success of the Iranian Revolution? These people who had no material resources at their disposal whatever, faced with one of the best-equipped armies in the world, opposed by all the major powers, and some of the lesser ones, nevertheless triumphed. How? The historians will still be scratching their heads a hundred years from now wondering how it happened. But the Muslim when he sees this will see the kind of leadership provided by Imam Khomeini and the moral and spiritual dimensions that he gave to the Iranian Revolution.

Question: What is the relationship between the *ulama* and the existing rulers of Iraq compared to the *ulama* of Iran?

HA: This is a subject on which I am not well informed. Recently there has been considerable antagonism between the Ba'athist regime in Iraq and Ayatullah Muhammad Baqir as-Sadr, who has been a close associate of Imam Khomeini and was an acquaintance of his during his long years in exile.[8] There are many reports of large-scale demonstrations in Iraq against the Ba'athist regime, which led to the killing of a large number of people and the arrest of many more, including the personal emissary of Imam Khomeini. I believe that the emissary was later released. There is a danger when we talk about the coming influence or even the present influence of the Iranian Revolution to think only in terms of Shi'i communities. Obviously Shi'i communities have a particular interest in what is going on in Iran, particularly those in Iraq, which is next door. But the influence of the Revolution is in no way confined to the various Shi'i communities.

Questioner (as above): I was talking in a historical sense.

---

[8] Ayatullah Muhammad Baqir as-Sadr was martyred by the Iraqi regime on April 8, 1980.

HA: Historically, the Shi'i element of Iraq led a long struggle against the British mandate. Ayatullah Kashani and his father, Mustafa Kashani, were sentenced to death by the British in Iraq for their role in opposing the imposition of a British regime there. Further, the Shi'i *ulama* also opposed the British in Iraq. There was a long and protracted *jihad* against the British regime. In the postwar period there was activism against the Hashimites and even more recently against the Ba'athists. But I am not in a position to go into details on the case of Iraq.

Question: The *mujtahids* can arrive at different conclusions based on different interpretations. All might be correct. No one can claim that he is right. You mentioned that various Imams said that no one should follow blindly a ruler. They should know what the reason was behind their rulings. How does that apply to what you have said about the *mujtahid*, the *marja'-i taqlid*?

HA: *Taqlid* is not following blindly. *Taqlid* is a recognition of the limits of one's own knowledge and competence, with respect to the practical injunctions (*furu'*) of Islamic jurisprudence, in the sense of the prophetic *hadith*, that Allah has mercy on the man who knows his limits and stops at them. There is a great exercise of judgement here when it comes to the choice of a particular *mujtahid* or the choice of a *marja'-i taqlid*. Having made that choice, you follow the guidance of someone who has more authority because of his degree of specialized learning. There is no question of blind following. Within the Shi'i school it is true that whatever result is arrived at has no claim to infallibility. It is a reasoned supposition. What is essential is not to follow the guidance of any given *mujtahid*; it is essential from the viewpoint of the Usuli school of thought that one should choose a certain *mujtahid*. To my mind this is one reason why our brethren in Iran have a far clearer understanding and sense of direction in their Islamic lives because they have this comprehensive leadership and guidance. Many people in the Sunni Muslim world unfortunately under the influence of Wahhabism and other related misfortunes, tend to reject *taqlid* without in any way approaching the position of the *mujtahid* themselves. It is a question of following the guidance and direction given by one who is obviously better qualified, than we are ourselves.

SECOND LECTURE

Imam Khomeini:
the embodiment of
a tradition

الٱللسٱللٱقالٱطٱلٱٱلٱلٱلٱق

The Islamic Revolution differs from other events of the present century that have been given the designation "revolution" by being firmly rooted in history. Far from being a radical break with the essential and profound developments of the Iranian nation, it is on the contrary a continuation and fruition of long years of political, spiritual, and intellectual development.

I laid particular stress last week on the development of the institution of the Shi'i *ulama*, beginning with their migration to Iran in the Safavid period. Then I described their gradual emergence as a class providing not only religious leadership in the narrow and technical sense but also leadership of a national and political nature, given increasingly to contesting the authority monarchical institution.

Inevitably I was obliged to omit certain topics and names, and by way of introduction to today's topic -- the culminating figure of this whole tradition of the *ulama*, Imam Khomeini -- I would like to make more detailed reference to some aspects of what I briefly touched upon last week.

First, it would obviously be a distortion of the institution of the *ulama* to regard it simply from the viewpoint that most interests us today -- namely, the political. We should bear in mind that the *ulama*, not only within the Shi'i and Iranian context, have been the guardians above all of a certain body of traditional learning and devotion that has been the whole underpinning and basis of social and political action.

If we look at the specific case of the Shi'i school of thought in Iran, we see that again since the early Safavid period -- beginning in the sixteenth century of the Christian era -- the *ulama* have studied and cultivated a wide variety of different disciplines. These have included not merely the familiar theological disciplines of Qur'an, *hadith*, *tafsir*, *fiqh*, and so on -- but philosophy, a certain form of philosophy appropriate to the Islamic context; and mysticism, again a certain form of mysticism appropriate to the Islamic and specifically the Shi'i context.

Indeed, if we look at the person of Imam Khomeini and his achievement, we find that he is the culmination of the tradition of the Shi'i *ulama* in Iran, not merely in exercising an unusually comprehensive, wide, and profound influence in political and social affairs, but also with respect to the purely learned dimension of the tradition. Here, too, he is an unparalleled figure.

This, then, is one thing. In order to understand the Islamic Revolution in Iran and the role played in it by the *ulama*, particularly Imam Khomeini, it is necessary to consider not merely their political theory, not merely their sensibility and strategy and their identification with popular aspirations, but also the background of cultivation of Islamic learning and piety from which they sprang.

Secondly, as a footnote to last week's presentation, I would like to go into more detail on two figures who provide the immediate background to the emergence of Imam Khomeini. The first is Shaykh 'Abd Al-Karim Hairi and the second is Ayatullah Burujirdi. The first is of great importance as the reviver of the religious learning institution in Qum, from which Imam Khomeini went forth and which has become in a certain sense the main stronghold of the Islamic Revolution in Iran and also the spiritual capital of the country, given the residence there of Imam Khomeini.

Qum is one of the oldest centers of Shi'i school of thought in Iran. Not coincidentally, it is also one of the few cities in Iran by where Arabs settled in large numbers. It has traditionally been a stronghold of Shi'i learning. However, until the present century the major centers of Shi'i learning that exercised great authority within Iran were generally situated outside the country in the cities known as the 'atabat -- that is, the cities of Iraq where certain of the imams are buried: Karbala, Kazimayn and above all Najaf. Almost all the prominent *ulama* received their essential education in Iraq. Many, even though Iranian by birth, would spend most of their lives there.

This situation has continued to a certain extent, but in Iran the city of Qum came to great prominence as a result of the activities of a succession of important *ulama*, the first of whom was Shaykh 'Abd Al-Karim Hairi (1859-1936). In 1922 he founded in the city what is known as the Hauza-yi 'Ilmiya, which roughly translated is "the teaching institution." It is a conglomerate of different colleges and institutions of learning, informally organized and containing a number of teachers, offering the entire spectrum of the traditional religious sciences, joined by philosophy and mysticism.

There is a tradition, attributed to the sixth imam of the Shi'a, that in latter times knowledge would arise in Qum and be distributed from there to the rest of Iran and to the rest of the Islamic world. Shaykh 'Abd Al-Karim Hairi, in fulfillment of this tradition, consciously decided to revitalize Qum as a center of religious learning and teaching. This took place in 1922, a couple of years before the foundation of the Pahlavi dictatorship. Although Shaykh 'Abd Al-Karim Hairi was consistently apolitical, it can be said that his achievement indirectly contributed to the ultimate overthrow and destruction of the Pahlavi dynasty.

Although he failed to exercise any effective opposition to Reza Khan and the institution of the Pahlavi dictatorship, Shaykh 'Abd Al-Karim Hairi came to repent his inactivity in this respect.

The second of these two figures who form the immediate background to the emergence of Imam Khomeini, is of course Ayatullah Burujirdi (1875-1962). He is the major *mujtahid* and *marja'-i taqlid* of the immediate postwar period. He continued the twin emphases of Shaykh 'Abd Al Karim Hairi -- the strengthening of the teaching institution in Qum as the center of spiritual and religious direction and a certain quietism in political affairs. He organized a network throughout Iran for the collection of *zakat, khums,* and other religiously sanctioned taxes, which gave a greater financial independence and stability to the religious institution in Qum. The network established for these purposes later became of great utility in the course of the Islamic Revolution. At the same time, Ayatullah Burujirdi on the purely religious plane instituted an important development which has not received sufficient attention -- a deliberate attempt by the leading authorities of Shi'i Muslims to affect a rapprochement with the Sunni Islamic world. Through his efforts and those of the then Shaykh al-Azhar, Shaykh Mahmud Shaltut, an institution was established for *taqrib,* the rapprochement between the different schools of thought in Islam. This theme has also been taken up by Imam Khomeini, who has repeatedly expressed the need for collaboration and unity between the different segments of the Islamic world.

Politically, however, Ayatullah Burujirdi was open to considerable criticism. Throughout the tumultuous events of the first decade of the postwar period, years that saw the rise of a large and threatening communist party in Iran, the Tudeh Party; the nationalization of the Iranian oil industry; the rise of Dr. Musaddiq; and the CIA coup d'etat, we find almost complete silence on the part of Ayatullah Burujirdi. Even after the royalist coup d'etat of August 1953, he received emissaries of the Shah's regime at his residence in Qum.

This seemed in the eyes of many Iranians to exclude any role for the *ulama,* for the religious leaders, in the opposition to the Shah's regime that was now intensifying after the downfall of the Musaddiq regime, particularly because the role of Ayatullah Kashani (d. 1962), one of the previous supporters of Dr. Musaddiq and the campaign for the nationalization of the Iranian oil industry, also seemed ambiguous on many points.

In the first years after the downfall of Dr. Musaddiq and the institution of the royal dictatorship under American patronage, we find a certain current of religiously inspired opposition to the Shah's regime. But it has no leading personality; it is relatively weak; and it is overshadowed by secular and leftist forms of opposition to the Shah's regime.

However, almost a decade after the overthrow of Musaddiq, in 1962 there emerges for the first time in prominence on the Iranian scene the great figure of Imam Khomeini. He overshadows not only all his predecessors in this tradition of *ulama* that I have attempted to sketch for you but also the figure of Musaddiq himself and certainly all other secular politicians and potential leaders of opposition to the royal regime.

The life of Imam Khomeini before his emergence in the public eye in 1962 deserves some attention.[1] As the final element in his name indicates, he was born in the little town of Khomeini in 1902 of a family that for many generations had cultivated religious knowledge and learning. His grandfather was a certain Sayyid Ahmad, who was also known as Sayyid Ahmad Hindi, because he had lived in India before settling in Iran.

The family was of Iranian origin, an earlier ancestor having migrated from Nishapur to India in the eighteenth century. Ultimately, since the Imam is a *sayyid* -- a descendant of the Prophet -- the origins of the family of course go beyond Iran. But throughout recent generations the family is Iranian. It is simply that one branch was established in India.

There are apparently even now a number of relatives of the family who are still resident there, somewhere near Lucknow. The Imam's father was Sayyid Mustafa Khomeini, who was killed at the behest of one of the richest landowners in the region some five months after the birth of the Imam, because, it is said, of his attempts to defend the impoverished peasantry.

---

[1] On the first sixty years in the life of the Imam, see now my article, "Imam Khomeini, 1902-1962: The Pre-Revolutionary Years," in *Islam, Politics, and Social Movements*, eds. I. Lapidus and E. Burke, University of California Press: Berkeley, 1988, pp. 263-288. For an overall sketch of his life, see my article, "Imam Khomeini: A Brief Biography," *Jurnal Pengajian Arab dan Tamadun Islam* (Bangi, Malaysia), I (1420/1999), pp. 3-37.

The learned and religious career of Imam Khomeini began when he was 17, in the year 1919, when he went to study in the city of Arak. After a brief stay he left this relatively small and unimportant city to go to the main center of religious learning in Iran, namely, Qum. His arrival followed the establishment there of the Hauza-yi Ilmiya by Shaykh 'Abd Al-Karim Hairi. Imam Khomeini swiftly emerged as one of his most promising younger students. Under his guidance, Imam Khomeini studied the disciplines of *fiqh* and *usul al-fiqh*, and at the same time he learned philosophy and mysticism under the guidance of several prominent teachers of the day, culminating in Mirza Muhammad Ali Shahabadi.

I would like to make a brief diversion to speak of the place of philosophy and mysticism in the learned and even the political career of Imam Khomeini. It is one of the remarkable facts about him that his political role in leading a revolution, unparalleled in recent history, has come totally to overshadow his achievements as a scholar, philosopher, and mystic. All too frequently in the modern Muslim mentality philosophy and mysticism are held to represent a retreat from reality, a total abdication of any kind of political and social role, as if they were merely abstract matters that had no real connection with the existing problems of Muslims and the Islamic world. Imam Khomeini is living proof that these two subjects, correctly conceived and pursued, are on the contrary the mainspring for a form of activity that is profoundly correct, guided by a clear insight that is not merely political and strategic but is at the same time an insight that is metaphysically correct and well guided.

As for mysticism in particular, it may be said that it is precisely the moral and spiritual qualities that Imam Khomeini has cultivated that have made him what he most obviously is -- a complete embodiment of the human ideal of Islam. This is a revolutionary leader who lives not in comfortable apartments but in the simplest circumstances, who spends his nights in prayer and supplication, whose daily sustenance consists of the simplest and most elementary foods. It seems to me that even his very thorough grounding in philosophy and mysticism has been of political relevance and effectiveness.

The earliest fame of Imam Khomeini in the teaching institution at Qum was precisely as an exponent of these two disciplines, philosophy and mysticism. He gave a number of well-attended lectures on some of the major texts of Islamic philosophy and developed great eloquence and a forceful teaching style. He also wrote in this period a number of texts, partly original and partly commentaries upon existing texts, which for the most part have remained unpublished. He also wrote a large number of books on *fiqh*, and came to be regarded as an authority in that field. Had his attainments been restricted to these relatively traditional area -- *fiqh* on the one hand and philosophy and mysticism on the other -- he would no doubt have entered the spiritual history of Iran as a great personality. But although in many respects he is the perpetuator, the culmination of a tradition, he also broke sharply with the existing tradition of the learned institution by cultivating from a quite early point radical political interests.

Shortly after the fall of Reza Khan, Imam Khomeini authored a book which was in large part a criticism of the Pahlavi dictatorship, entitled *Kashf al-Asrar* (*The Uncovering of Secrets*). It was uncompromising and clear, written in the same style that characterizes all his pronouncements. He vigorously criticized the regime of Reza Khan and laid open its dependence upon and subordination to foreign powers, at that time primarily Britain. He clearly saw that the hostility of the Pahlavi regime to Islam was not merely the idiosyncratic desire of a single dictator but rather part of a comprehensive strategy for the elimination of Islam as a social and political force throughout the Islamic world, and as such had been conceived by the major centers of imperialism and entrusted to the various local agents of imperialism.

In the course of the *Kashf al-Asrar,* he wrote, for example, in criticizing Reza Khan:

> All the orders issued by the dictatorial regime of the bandit Reza Khan have no value at all. The laws passed

by his parliament must be scrapped and burned. All
the idiotic words that have proceeded from the brain of
that illiterate soldier are rotten and it is only the law of
God that will remain and resist the ravages of time.

This form of expression, totally uncompromising and marked
by a radical insight into the realities of politics, gave rise to mis-
givings, interestingly enough not only on the part of the Pahlavi
regime but within the religious institution itself. For all its
strength, like any other institution it had as its primary interest
self-preservation and the promotion of its institutional concerns.

In the period when Ayatullah Burujirdi was the dominant figure in Qum, Imam Khomeini was gradually gaining in importance, but he still lacked the seniority that would have made his
views fully authoritative. It may have been in part for this reason
that in the period between the downfall of Reza Khan in 1941 and
the overthrow of Musaddiq in 1953, Imam Khomeini did not
attempt an open denunciation of the regime in the same fashion
as he did after 1963. He has more recently expressed regret that he
did not earlier begin on the course that for many years now he has
seen to be his clear and manifest duty. It has been said, however,
that throughout this period he sought to induce a measure of
political realism and commitment in Ayatullah Burujirdi. If his
efforts in this respect were largely frustrated, there is no doubt that
he exercised his influence upon a large number of the younger
ulama in Qum and elsewhere who later came to form part of the
directive force of the Revolution. Long before the beginning of the
revolutionary movement, he had built up a considerable following
among the younger *ulama* in Qum, many of whom are now
among the important leaders of the Revolution. It is highly prob-
able that the Council of the Islamic Revolution in Iran consists
largely of the pupils of Imam Khomeini. In other words, they are
people whom he has been training for years, in both the traditional religious sciences and the tasks of political struggle and guidance and leadership. A list of the major students of Imam
Khomeini would take many pages. We can mention briefly simply

two names that come to mind -- Imam Musa Sadr, the leader of the Shi'i community in Lebanon; and Ayatullah Muntaziri, who was one of the major strugglers against the Shah's regime in Iran.

Imam Khomeini's emergence to prominence in the political sphere began less than a decade after the overthrow of Musaddiq and the emergence of an intensified form of dictatorship in Iran. The first issue on which the Imam confronted the Iranian government was its proposal in the fall of 1962 to issue new laws governing elections to local and provincial councils, laws which were liable to permit Baha'is openly to hold office for the first time. More significantly, early the following year, the Shah inaugurated what became known in the western press, and of course in domestic propaganda, as the White Revolution. It has been appositely said of the White Revolution that the only white thing about it was that it was conceived in the White House. It was certainly not white in the sense that it was bloodless, and it was hardly a revolution. On the contrary, it was an attempt to forestall revolution and make it impossible.

The so-called White Revolution consisted of a package of measures allegedly designed to reform Iranian society to promote the welfare of the peasantry and the industrial workers and to "emancipate" the women. Among the various measures included in it there were two that assumed particular prominence in the propaganda of the Shah's regime and his foreign supporters -- land reform and women's rights. It may be appropriate to dwell a little on the nature of these two measures before continuing with my narrative of Imam Khomeini's activities.

The slogan of land reform in Iran was the disguise for the total disruption of the agrarian economy in a manner designed to assure maximum profit for the royal family; a certain oligarchy tied to the royal family; and foreign agribusiness interests, including companies headquartered in the United States, Europe, and Israel. It is true that a certain amount of property was distributed among the peasantry, but the land that was distributed was not always of cultivable nature and, moreover, it was not distributed free of charge; it was distributed against monetary payments that had to be made to banks controlled by the royal family. Moreover, large tracts of land were totally excluded from the scope of the law and were passed instead either to the direct ownership of the royal family under the title of the Pahlavi Foundation, which was the cover for the financial operations of the royal family, or certain foreign agribusiness interests that used the agrarian land of Iran for the cultivation of crops that were not consumed in Iran but were destined for the foreign market. For example, areas were given over to the cultivation of asparagus, an item totally missing from the Iranian diet. At the same time, Iranian-produced butter became increasingly unavailable, so that in a Tehran supermarket you could find only Danish butter.

This destruction of the agrarian economy caused massive depopulation of the countryside and migration to the cities of peasants forced to seek work. The former landowning class was transformed into speculators on urban real estate and import-export merchants, and in pure financial terms they generally gained from the transformation rather than lost from it.

As for women's rights, this was a measure designed more for foreign consumption than for domestic purposes, since the Shah's foreign advisers were well aware of the traditional western prejudices concerning Islamic attitudes towards women and thought that this was an infallible way of making the Shah appear an enlightened and benevolent person, acting on behalf of the poor oppressed women of Muslim Iran. In point of fact there has taken place a great transformation in the political-social role of women in Iran over the past fifteen years, but the direction it has taken is against the regime. Iranian women found their emancipation not through any measures decreed by the regime but on the contrary in struggling against the regime, in suffering abuse, torture, imprisonment, and martyrdom at the hands of the regime.

In the declarations of Imam Khomeini made from January 1963 onwards against the Shah's regime and his attempt to deceive Iranian opinion with the so-called White Revolution, we do not find consistent mention of land reform and women's rights. It is a remarkable thing that right down until last year it was said particularly in the American press -- and probably the British press was not much better -- that these conservative, reactionary, fanatical Muslims in Iran were struggling against the Shah because of their opposition to land reform and their desire to get back what was quaintly termed "the church lands" and because they wanted all women to be excluded from public life. This total absurdity has no basis, neither for the Revolution of the past year nor for the preceding fifteen years.

In the earliest declarations of Imam Khomeini, made in 1963, declarations that have been preserved verbatim and are available to anyone who can read Persian, he concentrates by contrast on a number of other themes. The first is the continued violation by the Shah of the Iranian constitution and his violation of the oath that he took upon acceding to the throne to preserve and to protect Islam. Secondly, he attacks the Shah's subordination to foreign powers, mentioning primarily the United States and, following very closely upon that, Israel.

The question of Israel with respect to the Islamic Revolution is of great importance. It has not been realized, because of the embargo on news in the so-called free press of the West, that Israel has been second only to the United States as one of the major props of the Pahlavi dictatorship. It was widely known in Iran that there were two items that were totally excluded from any form of public comment or criticism. It was a well-known rule of SAVAK, the security police established by the United States for the Shah, that there were two items that had to be totally excluded from public comment and criticism. One was the royal family and the other was Israel. It is interesting that even the United States, in a certain form and under certain pretexts, might be subjected to criticism, but even the name of Israel had not to be mentioned.

Imam Khomeini, with his characteristic refusal to compromise, broke this rule in 1963 and pointed out the very close relationship on the military, political, intelligence, and economic planes between the Pahlavi regime and Israel. Of course, in Western press reports at the time you would find not a word on this aspect of the matter.

As for land reform and women's emancipation, which were supposedly targets of so much righteous anger, the only references in the declarations of Imam Khomeini in 1963 and subsequently are passing references denouncing them as totally fallacious and not even worth commenting upon in detail.

In order to exact vengeance for the Imam's condemnation of his so-called reform program, the Shah had his paratroopers assault the Fayziya *madrasa* in Qum, the center of the Imam's activity, resulting in the death of a number of people. Completely unintimidated, the Imam continued his attacks on the regime, and on April 1 he condemned the persistent silence of certain conservative *ulama* as tantamount to collaboration with the Shah. Two days later, on the fortieth day after the attack on the Fayziya *madrasa*, he described the Iranian government as determined to eradicate Islam, at the behest of America and Israel, and himself as resolved to combat it.

Two months later, with the onset of Muharram, always a time of heightened religious awareness, the Imam made an ominous comparison of the Shah with the Umayyad caliph, Yazid, the murderer of Imam Husayn – upon whom be peace – , and he warned the Shah that if he did not change his ways the day would come when he would have to flee the country amid popular rejoicing. The warning was remarkably prescient, for this is precisely what happened on January 16, 1979. The immediate effect was, however, that the Imam was arrested two days later by commandos who descended on his house in Qum at 3 o'clock in the morning and took him to Tehran.

As dawn broke, the news of the Imam's arrest spread quickly, sparking a massive uprising in a number of cities, which was brutally repressed by the use of force. Not for the first time in the Shah's career he gave the orders to his security police and to the troops to shoot to kill. It has been estimated that by the time the uprising had been crushed, some six days later, approximately 15,000 people had been killed. The movement inaugurated by the uprising -- known as the movement of 15 Khurdad, after the day in the Iranian calendar on which it had begun -- was in an important sense the prelude to the Islamic Revolution of 1978-1979, in that the goals of that revolution -- the liberation of Iran from monarchical tyranny and its foreign patrons -- and its leadership had already been determined.

After a period of imprisonment and confinement in Tehran, Imam Khomeini was released and permitted to return to Qum on April 7, 1964. Officially inspired rumors had begun to circulate that the Imam had come to an "understanding" with the Shah's regime during his confinement. He swiftly dispelled these rumors after returning to Qum by declaring that the movement inaugurated on 15 Khurdad would continue.

Matters came to a head once more in the fall of the same year when the Shah concluded a status of forces agreement with America that provided immunity from prosecution for all American personnel in Iran and their dependents. This caused the Imam to deliver what was perhaps the most vehement of his speeches to date in denouncing the Shah. Were the dog of an American soldier to bite the Shah himself, the Shah would have no legal recourse, he declared. The Imam denounced the agreement as a surrender of Iranian independence and sovereignty, made in exchange for a $200 million loan that would benefit only the Shah and his associates, and described as traitors all those in the Majlis who voted to ratify it.

Shortly before dawn on November 4, 1964, the Imam was arrested again, and this time taken directly to Mehrabad airport in Tehran for immediate deportation to Turkey. He was compelled to reside first in Ankara and then in Bursa. The decision to deport rather than arrest Imam Khomeini and imprison him in Iran was based no doubt on the hope that in exile he would fade from popular memory. Physical elimination would have been fraught with the danger of an uncontrollable popular uprising. The choice of Turkey as destination   reflected the security cooperation then existing between Turkey and Iran, which together with Israel then formed the three main pillars on which American hegemony in the Middle East rested.

In September 1965 Imam Khomeini was enabled to leave his place of exile in Turkey to go to a more congenial environment, that of Najaf, one of the cities in Iraq that have traditionally been centers not only for the cultivation of Shi'i learning but of refuge for Iranian religious leaders. This was the case, for example, in the nineteenth century and early twentieth century when a number of the important religious leaders supported the constitutional revolution or, before that, the tobacco boycott movement. They issued their directives from the relative security of the *atabat*, which were outside Iran.

On this occasion, however, Imam Khomeini by no means found an untroubled refuge there. It needs to be pointed out very plainly and strongly that, despite what was said in the western press for many years, the presence of Imam Khomeini in Iraq in no way constituted any form of alliance, however slight, between himself and the Ba'athist regime in that country. He was, on the contrary, subjected to repeated harassment by the Ba'athists, in conjunction with the general repression enacted by the regime in Iraq, a repression that is continuing.

From Najaf, Imam Khomeini continued periodically to issue his declarations on Iranian affairs. The Shah's hope that exile would put an end to his influence and popularity was decisively frustrated. It has been said that Imam Khomeini emerged to prominence in the course of the Revolution as the result of a vacuum because there was no viable alternative in sight, but this judgment results from ignorance of the gradual development of the role of Imam Khomeini during his more than fourteen years in exile. Throughout his years in Najaf he by no means remained silent. We find him, on the contrary, issuing a wide variety of proclamations on Iranian affairs, all of which penetrated the country, were circulated, and had a growing effect on the formation of Iranian public opinion.

For example, in April 1967 Imam Khomeini sent an open letter to the prime minister of Iran, Amir 'Abbas Hoveyda, in which he denounced Hoveyda and the Shah for their continued violation both of Islam and of the constitution. He went through a comprehensive survey of all the government's policies, criticizing them one by one, warning Hoveyda that one day he would be held responsible. One may imagine the contemptuous disbelief with which Hoveyda received this letter from an exile whose followers had been slaughtered in the streets, a letter addressed to the prime minister at the head of one of the major repressive apparatuses in the modern world. Yet one of the remarkable things about Imam Khomeini, which contributes to the effectiveness of his leadership, is that every word he has said is seriously meant. This warning, given as far back as April 1967, bore its fruit with the execution of Hoveyda by the Islamic Revolutionary Court in the aftermath of the Revolution.

Another example of the declarations of Imam Khomeini during his years in exile we can draw from a series of events in May 1970 when a consortium of American investors met in Tehran to discuss ways for the more effective penetration and exploitation of the Iranian economy. On this occasion one of the followers of the Imam, Ayatullah Saidi, gave a *khutba* in his mosque in Tehran denouncing this conference and calling upon the Iranian people to rise up and protest against it. He was arrested and tortured to death by SAVAK, the Shah's security police, and Imam Khomeini issued a proclamation calling on the people to renew their struggle against the Pahlavi regime.

Later, we find Imam Khomeini denouncing the idiotic and wasteful expenditures of the regime for the so-called celebration of twenty-five hundred years of monarchy, a celebration conceived and planned by certain Israeli advisers of the regime. He later also condemned the inauguration of a one-party system in Iran, saying that whoever joined this party voluntarily, without pressure, was in effect a traitor to both the nation and Islam. He also issued many proclamations on the general state of the Islamic world and in particular on the role of Israel.

It is interesting to note that on at least two occasions, once in 1971 and once during the Revolution, Imam Khomeini also issued two appeals to the Muslim world in general, appeals that were translated into various languages and distributed during the *Hajj.*

In both these declarations he called for solidarity among the Muslims and collaboration for the solution of their common problems. It is interesting to note that the so-called champion of Islam, the Saudi regime, saw fit to imprison and torture for long periods a number of those responsible for the distribution of these declarations. Therefore, it was no surprise to anyone that the Saudi regime, despite its professed loyalty to Islam, ranged itself with Israel, the United States, and the Soviet Union in opposing the Islamic Revolution. It has a long history of opposition to the revolutionary Islamic movement led by Imam Khomeini.

Throughout the years of Imam Khomeini's exile in Najaf, during which he was receiving visitors from Iran and making these and other proclamations on Iranian and Islamic affairs in general, a number of important developments were taking place in Iran that also contributed to the Revolution. Foremost among these was the lecturing and writing activity of the subject of my next lecture, Dr. Ali Shari'ati. I can say in partial anticipation that his influence on a different plane acted as a complement to that of Imam Khomeini. The massive and overwhelming response given by the Iranian people during the Revolution to the declarations and leadership of Imam Khomeini is in part due to the undeniable influence of Dr. Shari'ati during the years of Imam Khomeini's exile.

As for the role of Imam Khomeini in the Revolution itself, this is direct and immediate in the sense that the opening events of the Revolution are directly concerned with his person. The government-controlled press in January 1978 published an article insulting Imam Khomeini in abusive and obscene terms. That aroused an immediate response of anger in the city of Qum. After the first uprising in Qum, which was suppressed with heavy loss of life, a series of demonstrations and protests unfurled across Iran with ever increasing tempo, until December 1978 when probably the greatest demonstrations not merely in Iranian history but of modern history in general took place, forcing the exiling of the Shah soon after and paving the way for the ultimate triumph of the Revolution.

Imam Khomeini increased the tempo of his declarations as the movement picked up speed within Iran. In October of last year (1978) he was expelled from Iraq as a result of an agreement between the Shah's regime and the Ba'athist regime. It is interesting to note that Imam Khomeini considered a number of possible alternatives. He would have preferred to take up residence in a Muslim country but, as he said publicly, and as I myself have heard from him, not one Muslim country offered him the possibility of a residence that would be safe and permit him to continue his activity. This simple fact is an eloquent commentary on the nature of the regimes that rule the different Muslim countries today. The Qur'an orders the Muslims to give refuge even to a *mushrik* in order that he might hear the Qur'an and be informed of religion. Yet these contemporary Muslim regimes that send money for the construction of mosques, preferably in prestige places like London, New York, and so on; that hold conferences in Hilton and Sheraton hotels, refuse even the elementary right of security and refuge to one whom any objective Muslim observer must regard as the greatest *mujahid* of the present day.

Like so many of the stratagems of the former Iranian regime, this one also turned against it in its ultimate result, because faced with the impossibility of finding refuge in any other Muslim country after Iraq, Imam Khomeini proceeded to Paris, where he became infinitely more accessible to Iranians from America, Europe, and Iran itself. He also became immediately accessible to the world press -- not that the world press, of course, was in any way inclined or even intellectually and mentally equipped to reflect the true message and aspirations of Imam Khomeini. Nonetheless, from Paris his communications with Iran were infinitely easier and his visibility was far greater than had been the case in Najaf.

The study of the proclamations of Imam Khomeini during the year of the Revolution would in itself be an interesting topic. One sees throughout the year as the Revolution reaches new peaks a certain evolutionary style of his declarations. For example, if one looks at the declaration he issued on the eve of Muharram last year

(A. H. 1399, December 1978), one sees a great eloquence and forcefulness of expression that one would say from a purely literary point of view has few parallels in contemporary Iranian expression. By the time he returned to Iran from exile at the beginning of February this year (1979), Imam Khomeini, with no material resources, without the construction of a political party, without the waging of a guerrilla war, without the support of a single foreign power, had established himself as the undisputed leader of a major revolutionary movement.

How is that possible? I shall try to supply part of the answer in my fourth lecture, in which I shall examine the events and the chronology of the Revolution and certain general conclusions that can be drawn. Now, with respect to the person of Imam Khomeini, I would suggest the following concerning his importance as a revolutionary leader.

First, the "Revolution" for him -- and I use quotation marks because the word has all kinds of connotations that are not necessarily appropriate to the Iranian context -- is one in which as a revolutionary leader he is not merely intellectually and emotionally committed to a certain cause but is totally identified with it. He has been totally unwilling to compromise. Why? It is because he has not been a politician of a familiar kind, concerned with the attainment of personal political advantage. On the contrary, he has simply sought to heed the commands of Allah and His Messenger in a fashion that he has deemed appropriate to the circumstances.

One of my Iranian acquaintances who travelled to Paris to visit Imam Khomeini asked him; "Do you think our present course is wise? What will happen if the army keeps on slaughtering people? Will people sooner or later not get tired and discouraged?" He responded quite simply that it is our duty to struggle in this fashion and the result is with Allah. It is precisely this apparent lack of strategy, this refusal to contemplate the precise calculations of normal political strategy, that constitute the highest form of revolutionary strategy in an Islamic context.

Secondly, we can say that Imam Khomeini has been enabled to fulfill the great and unparalleled role that he has by his spiritual and moral qualities, qualities that cannot be called into doubt by even those who have ideologically no commitment to Islam. One of the remarkable things is that in the course of the Revolution, people who had no particular commitment to Islam in an ideological fashion came to rediscover Islam and at the same time made a commitment to it as a revolutionary force because of the self-evident moral and spiritual virtues of Imam Khomeini himself. It was obvious that here was a man in no way concerned with the obtaining of a personal or sectarian benefit, but one who represented the deepest aspirations of the Iranian nation.

Discussion

Question: You mentioned the important role of philosophy and mysticism. Could you elaborate on this slightly, specifically in relation to Sufism? I do not know whether in the Shi'i school of thought, Sufism is organized as it is in the Sunni world. If so, the question of Imam Khomeini's affiliation would be important.

HA: The word *mysticism* is a little problematical. I used it for convenience as an English approximation. Sufism as an organized body has only a peripheral existence in Shi'i school. We do find Sufi orders, but they are generally rejected by the Shi'i *ulama*. What I mean by mysticism with respect to Imam Khomeini is what is known as *'irfan*, which is a different form of mysticism appropriate to the Shi'i context. This is something that draws upon certain dimensions of the Qur'an, the teachings of the Twelve Imams of the Ahl al-Bayt (upon whom be peace), we well as concept; and formulations of Ibn 'Arabi. This is what I mean by mysticism in this context -- a form of mystical devotion that gives a certain contour to the spiritual life. It has clearly given Imam Khomeini -- I do not like to use the expression, but for want of a better one -- a certain otherworldliness. It is a paradox that here one has a man so devoid of worldly ambition who is yet on a worldly plane so eminently successful. Viewing matters at a deeper level, from the viewpoint of Islam, we see that it is not a paradox at all. The rejecting by the self of all forms of attachment to this world makes it possible to be extremely effective and active in this world. In that sense of the *hadith*, he who humbles himself before Allah will be raised by Allah. This is what I intended by the reference to mysticism in Imam Khomeini.

Question: Will you please explain the concept of the *imam* and the concept of the caliph, and the relationship between the two, with particular emphasis on two points -- the unity of the *ulama* and, secondly, in relation to the contemporary situation in Iran?

HA: This is a very wide question, not directly related to today's talk. I am sure that most of the audience know what is implied in the terms *imam* and *caliph*. The imam in the Shi'i school is the divinely appointed leader of the community, the first of whom is 'Ali and the last of whom is the Twelfth Imam, who is held to be in a state of *ghayba*, of occultation, of absence from the physical plane, but nonetheless continues to exercise his authority. This form of succession is in a sense hereditary. Moreover, the prerogatives of these appointed successors to the Prophet go beyond the purely political, administrative, military tasks of the caliph in Sunni thought.

I am not sure beyond that what it is possible to say without embarking on an unnecessarily detailed lecture. What is perhaps of more interest is the second part of your question, the relevance of these differences to the present day state of the Islamic world. I would say that it is minimal, if not nonexistent, since the Sunni Muslim countries do not have a caliph, nor does there exist a machinery or any conceivable process at present for the selection of a caliph. As far as Shi'ism is concerned, the imam is also in a state of *ghayba* so it does not pose itself as a problem.[2]

What both Sunni and Shi'i Muslims should direct their attention towards is collaboration on the far more numerous and important matters on which they are agreed. There is no doubt that the Islamic Revolution can be, and already to some extent has been, an important occasion for the gradual elimination of centuries of prejudice and hostility between Sunni and Shi'i.

Imam Khomeini himself, when I had the honor of meeting him in Paris, expressed a great sorrow that when the Shi'i Muslims of Iran were obtaining martyrdom in the streets of Tehran during the last Muharram for the sake of the establishment of an Islamic

---

[2] On reflection, I am bound to remark that my equation between the *ghayba* of the Twelfth Imam (may his reappearance be hastened) and the absence of a caliph tends to trivialize the distinction between the respective political predicaments of Shi'i and Sunni Muslims. For the *ghayba* does yield a coherent political theory, that of *vilayat-i faqih*, whereas the absence of a caliph has resulted simply in a vacuum.

republic, Shi'i and Sunni Muslims in India in the same month of Muharram were engaged in slaughtering each other because of the details of *ta'ziya*.

Fortunately, as a result of the Revolution one sees a large number of encouraging developments. For example, in Afghanistan, a country where there have been deep and prolonged hostilities between the Sunnis and Shi'i -- probably about seventy percent of the population are Sunni and thirty percent Shi'i -- one sees in the wake of the Islamic Revolution of Iran, and in the course of resistance to the Soviet-established Marxist regime, that historic hatreds have been overcome to a remarkable degree. They are fighting together against Soviet imperialism.[3] (This was before the Soviet invasion of December 1979.) In Turkey, again a country where because of centuries of warfare between the Ottomans and the Safavids there are deep-rooted prejudices towards the Shi'i school, a positive interest has been aroused as a result of the Revolution. In many Islamic periodicals in that country now one can see articles about Sunni-Shi'i relations, a desire to obtain objective, correct information about Shi'i school of thought and above all to establish an effective collaboration between the Islamic movement in that country and the Islamic Revolution in Iran.

Therefore, rather than hashing over again the question of *imam* and caliph or whatever differences may have existed, it is far more fruitful for Muslims to spend their energies in establishing closer links of cooperation. After all, we should not forget that the Islamic Revolution has been the only major setback to the cause of Zionism in the Middle East -- far more than any military undertaking attempted by any of the Arab States, far more even than the activities of the Palestinians themselves, however heroic these may have been. There can be no doubt that the only major setback suffered by Zionism and American imperialism in the entirety of the Middle East region -- or, if you like, the Muslim region -- has been the Islamic Revolution in Iran.

---

[3] Superfluous to point to the sorry truth that whatever sectarian or ethnic unity was fostered by the Afghan *jihad* has long since dissipated.

It is a Revolution that has potential in the service of all Muslims. It is up to the Muslims of the Sunni countries -- Arab countries, Turkey, Afghanistan and so on -- to align themselves with this Revolution and give it every possible form of support and cooperation.

Question: You mentioned Israel. What was the role of the Jewish minority in Iran in collaboration with Israel, in the light of the execution of one of their leaders?

HA: We should not make the automatic assumption that all of the Jewish minority in Iran was Zionist in its aspirations or aligned with the previous regime, the Pahlavi regime. Some certainly were. The millionaires like Elqanian, who was put to death, had very close ties with Israel and also with the regime.

But apart from the existence of the Jewish community in Iran, the state of Israel had very close ties with the Pahlavi regime, not necessarily through the Iranian Jewish community. Those ties were established, I think, in 1948 shortly after the establishment of the Zionist state in Palestine when de facto recognition was accorded to Israel by the Iranian government of the day. Despite his nationalist inclinations, Musaddiq failed to revoke that recognition.

Then a more thoroughgoing relationship between Israel and the Iranian government came into being after the coup d'etat in 1953. Cooperation took place on many levels, but notably in so-called intelligence and security work. After a certain point it appears that the task of staffing and training SAVAK was taken over from the CIA by Mossad, the Israeli security, although the CIA always retained the right of supervision over the operations of SAVAK. I know people who report having been interrogated and tortured by Israelis while in the custody of SAVAK. It was a deep involvement.

In return, the Israelis got a large proportion of their oil -- between seventy and ninety percent -- from Iran. There was a certain amount of penetration of the Iranian economy, partly through Iranian Jews, but not in all cases. The relationship with Israel was a corollary of the Shah's subservience to the United States.

The Shah's collaboration with Israel did not always go through the Jewish community. It also went through the Baha'i community. If one is speaking of minorities the most important one with respect to staffing the Shah's regime, staffing the bureaucracy and the security police, is the Baha'is, many of whom in any case are of Jewish origin. A number of cases could be mentioned, including the former vice-chief of SAVAK, Sabeti. He was of Jewish origin and received his training in torture techniques in Israel. He and a number of other officers are living in Israel after the Revolution. It is Baha'is rather than the Jews as a community who might be indicted in this respect.

Israel, with its eternal search for immigrants, thought that an ideal situation was developing in Iran with the Revolution. But apart from a certain minority that profited handsomely under the Pahlavi regime, the bulk of Iranian Jewry is not yet showing an interest in leaving the country to go to Israel.[4] That minority is interesting. There was a piece in the *Economist*, which one can hardly accuse of being anti-Semitic, describing the arrival in Israel of certain Iranian Jewish immigrants. As they unrolled their carpets at Tel Aviv airport, the gold tumbled out onto the tarmac. This was an interesting demonstration of the way in which this Jewish oligarchy was able to profit under the Pahlavi regime. However, the majority of Iranian Jews decided to remain behind, much to the displeasure of the Jewish Agency, which therefore began to have recourse to the same kind of subversive tactics it had earlier employed in certain Arab countries, notably Iraq, in order to provoke fear among Iranian jews. These tactics were uncovered and publicized by an organization in Tehran called the Society of

---

[4] Subsequently, of course, large numbers of Jews did leave Iran, although more frequently for Southern California than for Israel. A certain amount of return migration is said to have taken place, presumably as a result of disquiet with American mores.

Jewish Intellectuals, which warned members of the community against these Zionist tactics.

When I was in Paris in December and early January visiting Imam Khomeini, a delegation of Iranian Jews came to visit him, and on that occasion he assured them not merely that Iranian Jews should remain in the country but that those who had been deceived by Zionism and had migrated to Palestine where they were receiving treatment as second-class citizens because of their Asiatic and non-East European origins should return to Iran, where as citizens of the Islamic Republic they would enjoy rights superior to those they had in the Jewish state of Israel.

Question: What position was held by Imam Khomeini after he graduated from the institute of Qum? Did he introduce changes in the curriculum and methodology? I should also like to know whether his open criticism of the Shah's regime was on behalf of the *ulama* or of a particular group that he founded.

HA: As regards the methodology of teaching, I think it is true to say that in effect Imam Khomeini brought about a reform in that he established a close link between the subjects he was teaching and the practical concerns of the day. For this reason, he attracted a far larger audience than many of the other teachers in Qum.

There are a number of individuals who have attained importance in Qum in reforming, in strengthening, the teaching institution. Both Imam Khomeini and others have performed great services in this respect in making the teaching syllabus of greater applicability to present-day problems. As for your second question, I do not think that Imam Khomeini in 1963 or subsequently was speaking either on behalf of the *ulama* in particular or on behalf of a more narrow group. On the contrary, he saw it to be his duty as a scholar of Islam and a citizen of Iran to speak out on these problems. One of the constant themes of all his proclamations is that the *ulama* have a great importance and dignity in Islam that they cannot fulfill simply by the reading and teaching of texts; that they have a far more comprehensive duty, indicated in the *hadith* which describes them as the heirs of the prophets. They cannot effectively transmit the legacy of the prophets simply by retreating into the corner of a *madrasa* and reading and commenting on texts. They have a far more comprehensive duty of guidance. He was speaking as an *alim*, conscious of the comprehensive nature of his responsibility, but this is different from speaking on behalf of the *ulama* as a class. On the contrary, he addressed himself to the entirety of the Iranian nation and beyond that to Muslims at large.

Question: You referred to doubts about the role of Ayatullah Burujirdi and you mentioned Ayatullah Kashani. It seems to me that you are taking a unidirectional view of the Iranian *ulama*. You must have pointed out in your last lecture that the difficulty stems from the fact that there are various possible interpretations of the role of *ulama* during the *ghayba* of the Twelfth Imam. As is evident from Ayatullah Naini's (1860-1936) work, one is faced with the question of either leaving the political field altogether and waiting for the reappearance of the Imam on the physical plane or with devising a system that is the least imperfect.

If you take the two extremes, you can see that the various *ulama* have taken their stance somewhere between these, and therefore fashioned their own activities on the political plane in accordance with their interpretation of the *ghayba*. It seems to me that Ayatullah Burujirdi was very much in favor of a quietist attitude, although in present day circumstances apparently that attitude may seem indefensible. But if it is viewed in the context of the responsibility of the *ulama* during that *ghayba* of the Imam it may become more explicable. I should like your comments.

HA: It is not my intention to criticize Ayatullah Burujirdi or Kashani for the roles they played. I merely wished to point out in the historical context the effect of their attitudes or at least of the perception of their attitudes. It is true that there have been differences of opinion among Shi'i *ulama* as to the political implications of the *ghayba*. But the general belief that has acquired increasing force since the days of Ayatullah Burujirdi is what Imam Khomeini describes in his book as the *vilayat* (governance) of the scholar; the duty of leading and guiding the community devolves upon the scholar.

I feel unhappy that in the course of these lectures I am obliged to generalize and oversimplify. This is in the nature of the situation, but it should be pointed out at least that Imam Khomeini's position has evolved over the years.[5] Although he has certain very distinct characteristics from the very beginning, I would say that his political -- I would not like to use the word philosophy -- attitude has changed and evolved.

After all in 1963 he was calling not for the institution of an Islamic republic in Iran, but for the implementation of the existing constitution, which provided for a monarchy however limited in its exercise of power. He was calling upon the Shah in effect to observe and fulfill the oath that he had taken to observe the constitution and to be loyal to Islam. I would say that a progressive radicalization of Imam Khomeini's position took place in his years of exile, and more particularly in the course of the Revolution.

There are many things to be said here, and I would like to have had more time. But as you have raised this question of political theory, which is of importance, I think it is permissible to say that in the usage of Imam Khomeini there is a difference, at least implied, between an Islamic republic and an Islamic state.[6] On the

---

[5] Although a change took place in the public utterances of the Imam, away from an apparent conditional acceptance of monarchy to an uncompromising demand for its abolition, it is entirely possible that in his own mind he had come to reject its legitimacy several decades earlier.

[6] Although a change took place in the public utterances of the Imam, away from an apparent conditional acceptance of monarchy to an uncompromising demand for its abolition, it is entirely possible that in his own mind he had come to reject its legitimacy several decades earlier. The distinction I sought to establish here between "Islamic Republic" and "Islamic State," and the suggestion that the former was intended to be the precursor of the latter, arose largely from the newness at the time in the usage of the revolution of the expression "Islamic Republic;" it had not been used by the Imam in his Najaf lectures on Islamic government. However, although there was no presumption that the Islamic Republic would attain instant perfection in matters of governance, there was equally no indication that an imperfect "republic" was intended to be the forerunner of a less

one hand, an Islamic republic is intended to be a transitional form of government in which the policies of the state will be geared in a general fashion towards the objectives of Islam and the administration of the affairs of the state will be entrusted to committed Muslims. But there will not be a total implementation of Islamic law in every area of life.

At the same time this provisional form of government, which will bear the name of republic, is in existence, a process of education and enlightenment will take place with respect to both those who have been alienated from Islam and those whose Islam is of a narrowly traditional type -- that is, based on prayer, fasting, and so on, without much awareness of political and social issues.

When that process has been completed, the Islamic republic will be succeeded by the Islamic state. There is no explicit statement to this effect by Imam Khomeini, but it is an impression that can be gained from careful reading of his proclamations during the year of the new Revolution and after his return. That impression is strengthened by reading of the draft of the constitution. One of the interesting things about it is that it does not have any explicit statement that the laws of state are to be the laws of Islam. Of course, it is a draft constitution and it may be revised before it is finally ratified, but as it stands there is no explicit stipulation that the laws of the state should be the laws of Islam. Instead, there is a provision that we find in the constitution of a number of other Muslim countries that no legislation shall be enacted that is contrary to Islam, which is quite different.[7]

---

imperfect "state." The introduction of the term "Islamic Republic" into revolutionary discourse turns out simply to have been a device for underlining the abolition of the monarchy. More recently, President Khatami has taken it to imply a coequal role for the people in administering the system of rule as a complement to its Islamicity.

[7] The draft constitution, published in June 1979, was indeed subjected to extensive revision. The final version drawn up in November of the same year differed in several important respects from the draft, above all through the introduction of the key principle of *vilayat-i faqih*. My prediction of a deliberately gradual Islamization of the polity was based on the assumption that the draft constitution would not be substantially revised.

It seems to me that in the context of Iran this is intended as a transitional stage, a stage at which that which is repugnant to Islam will be gradually uprooted and an effort will be made to move in the direction of a truly integral Islamic state. Where things to that effect are to be found in other constitutions, notably that of Pakistan, it is a piece of demagoguery. But in the case of Iran -- I hope I am right, only events will tell -- the inclusion of this clause should be seen as a provisional measure. It would be easy to make an overnight declaration that now everything will be according to the *shari'a* and go around spectacularly chopping off hands, and so on. But I think that this is one measure of the seriousness of the Revolution and the authenticity of the process of gradualness that is being embarked upon. We can sum up this gradualness as being within the concept of an Islamic republic, which will be the prelude to an Islamic State.

Question: May I ask a supplementary question? In this evolution of Imam Khomeini's thought from pure implementation of the constitution to an Islamic state, do you think he has moved to a position that was taken up by Ayatullah Nuri way back during the constitutional revolution at the turn of the century and broken line with the constitutionalists altogether?[8]

HA: I do not think one can equate the position of Imam Khomeini with that of Shaykh Fazlullah Nuri, who was one of the leading *ulama* during the constitutional revolution in Iran in the first decade of the present century. Unlike many of his colleagues, Nuri came to oppose the constitution, on compelling religious grounds, although there is no denying that he allied himself tactically with the court. He put forward certain telling arguments in a number of theoretical writings against the constitution. His slogan was "We want *mashru'a* (*shari'a* government), not *mashruta* (constitutional government)." Although for many years it was customary in Iran in Islamic circles to deride Nuri and to regard him as a trai-

---

[8] "Constitution" in this question relates to the Iranian constitution of 1906-1907 which remained theoretically in force until the Islamic Revolution.

tor, a reactionary, and so on, it is true that a certain reappraisal of him has taken place giving him a more creditable position.

However, it is not helpful to suggest a parallel between him and Imam Khomeini for many reasons. The most obvious and most important is that he was content to see the monarchy continue and even tried to find a place for it, which is obviously not the case with Imam Khomeini.

Question: Nothing has been mentioned about the role of women in the Revolution. What was his view of the role of women in the Islamic struggle?

HA: There are two reasons why the role of women has not been mentioned. The first is that I have been talking about the *ulama* and Imam Khomeini. Secondly, "the role of women" is a phrase that I think Muslims should use with great caution. It is a phrase that has been coined by non-Muslims and often serves to distract us and waste our mental energies.

Once you speak about the role of women you have the role of men, as if there were a great divide, men and women doing totally different things. All that you can say with respect to the Islamic Revolution is that Iranian women together with Iranian men played a very important role in furthering the aims of the revolution. They participated massively in all the important demonstrations. They suffered torture, imprisonment, and abuse. Since the triumph of the revolution they have continued to play an important role.

It is interesting that a revolution that, according to the popular image in the western press, is designed to reduce women to a status of total inferiority should see this unique picture of Muslim women in their Muslim dress on the streets participating and guarding demonstrations, holding machine guns. It is enough to say that on Black Friday, 8 September 1978, when more than four thousand people were slaughtered in Tehran, to the applause of President Carter, among those slaughtered were a minimum of six hundred women.

Dr. Kalim Siddiqui: Those who write books on women in Islam should be asked, "When were women outside Islam?"

Question: In your course outline you put a heading "The Imam as Ruler." Would you like to expand on that?

HA: On reflection, I am not sure that the word *ruler* is appropriate in the context. What he has done in the aftermath of the Revolution is to continue in the same role as he predicted before the triumph of the Revolution -- that of the guide who speaks out whenever he feels it necessary on matters of policy. Since his guidance is of the nature that it will be immediately followed, he comes in effect to be the final arbiter in almost all matters that he chooses to speak on.

The nature of the guidance given by Imam Khomeini since the triumph of the Revolution in February (1979) has been to ensure that the Revolution's fundamental aims are kept intact and no major deviation takes place. Of course, the frequent complaint of the Iranian leftists and their allies, the rightist press of Britain and the United States, is that the old dictatorship has been replaced by a new one. There are a large number of fallacies in this comparison. We should point out that the authority of Imam Khomeini derives entirely from the popular will and the popular choice. If he "interferes" with the government's workings or issues directives, this should not be construed as illegitimate interference. On the contrary, the government of Mehdi Bazargan derives its authority because it was nominated by Imam Khomeini. The Muslim masses of Iran demanded the institution of an Islamic republic under the leadership of Imam Khomeini. Therefore his authority is precisely the authority brought into being by the will of the people. This is an exceptional and transitional situation. It is not something that one can say will be institutionalized in the future.[9]

---

[9] A clearly unjustified prediction, in defence of which it might be pointed out that in the summer of 1979 the final shape of the constitution of the Islamic Republic was still under discussion and the fundamental principle of *vilayat-i faqih* had not yet been taken for granted as its main operating principle.

Therefore, I do not think that the word *ruler* in the synopsis that I prepared in haste is appropriate. He continues to be the *leader*. I know that this is a word that has unfortunate connotations from different contexts, but one has little choice. He continues to be the leader of the Revolution in all senses.

Question: It is in that context that you use the word *imam* when you talk about him?

HA: Yes. In designating him as *imam* we should not imagine that the word is applied to him in the same sense as the Twelve Imams of Shi'i tradition.[10] I am not aware of the precise time when the term came to be applied to him by the Iranian people. Maybe some of our Iranian brothers here could enlighten us on that. I think that the title was given to him in the course of the revolution. It has come to be applied to him increasingly after the revolution and to supplant the title that has by now become familiar to the western press, namely, *Ayatullah*.

This usage of the word *imam* is, after all, justified on the condition that we do not confuse it with the Shi'i concept of imam, because his authority, his leadership, has gone far beyond that which has been traditionally exercised by an *ayatullah*. One of the things that I did not give myself a chance to mention is that, of course, Imam Khomeini is from one point of view a *mujtahid*. People have been following him because he is a *mujtahid*. But his authority has gone far beyond the traditional bounds of a *marja'-i taqlid* or *mujtahid*. He has been followed not merely in the traditional sense of *taqlid*, but in a far more comprehensive sense. This comprehensiveness of his leadership, which is indeed based on the whole concept of *taqlid* but has gone beyond it, is reflected in the use of the word *imam*. I should be interested to know precisely what our Iranian brothers understand by the word when they apply it to him.

Comment: It was newly introduced into our language. We never used such a word for a *mujtahid*. This is a reflection of the Islamic

---

10 This sense of the title imam implies, of course, the key attribute of inerrancy (*'ismat*), the enjoyment of continuous divine protection from error and sin.

teaching. This means a leader, political as well as spiritual. But this is very recent. It is because usually you find that *mujtahid* is not sufficient.

HA: In some publications from Iran. I have seen him described as *Naib al-Imam*, the vice-regent of the Hidden Imam. Is this very widespread?

Comment: Yes. It is being used by some people to indicate to others not to confuse the real meaning of *imam*.

Comment: Ayatullah Khomeini is *mujtahid and* and not an *imam*. The use of this term in Persian really began when he was in Paris. Since then people have started calling him *imam*. But this is not new. It happened before while he was in Iraq because he was in an Arab environment, and *imam* in Arabic literature means simply *the leader*, not a traditional Shi'i leader. They use the term for Musa Sadr, calling him Imam Musa Sadr, because he lives in Lebanon, in an Arab environment. The Shi'i term would be *mujtahid*.

HA: I think this is true.In some of the literature in Arabic one finds the use of the word in early days with respect to Imam Khomeini. But its introduction to Persian usage in Iran seems more recent.

Dr Kalim Siddiqui: About eighteen months ago we had a course on the political thought of Islam, and, as in all our courses, we had both Sunni and Shi'i participants. As individuals we are Sunnis and Shi'i, but as an institution we are just Muslim. During the discussion on the political thought of Islam, it emerged that if and when Muslims came to the point of establishing a modern Islamic state, the Shi'i and Sunni positions would be identical, that in their operational, practical form there would be no difference. Would you agree with this assessment?

HA: I think that in general terms this is without doubt true. If one were to list the major differences of belief or outlook between

Sunnis and Shi'ites, one would see that the most important relate to matters that have no immediate practical application. The whole question of the imamate, even though it is of great importance in the Shi'i perspective as long as the *ghayba* continues, would not arouse any problems of political collaboration with Sunnis.

If one looks at the other differences of a minor variety relating to the details of *fiqh,* one will see that some of the differences between the four (Sunni) *madhhabs* are greater than the differences that separate them from Ja'fari *fiqh.*

Therefore, as you phrase it, in the operational details of a functioning Islamic state there need be no fundamental difference between Sunni and Shi'i. If there be any, they will arise from the differing provisions not merely between Sunni and Shi'i but the four schools of the Sunni Muslims, insofar as they choose to bind themselves by the four schools.

Comment: Though there is certainly a historical and ideological difference between the imamate and caliphate, between Shi'i and Sunni schools, as far as the modern situation is concerned I do not think there are any ideological differences between the two. The question of leadership is the most important issue regarding the political affairs of a Muslim state. The basis of leadership in Shi'i jurisprudence is the religious-social responsibility *(wajib al-kifai),* which is shared currently by the Sunnis. They both base their authority on the doctrine of the *al-amr bi'l-ma'ruf wa al-nahy 'an al-munkar.*

Dr Kalim Siddiqui: This point is not generally understood and it needs to be brought home clearly.

Comment: I agree it should be explained. But the difficulty is this: How can we introduce a Khomeini-type leadership into Sunni communities?

Dr Kalim Siddiqui: Since the Revolution in Iran I have been moving around some of the Sunni countries -- some of the most reactionary Sunni countries, if I may put it that way. I can assure you that the people in those countries have been absolutely galvanized and their imaginations have been captured by the Revolution in Iran. Some of them take the precaution of locking their doors before they talk about it. If national boundaries were taken away, probably Imam Khomeini would be elected by acclamation by the *ummah* as a whole as the leader of the Muslim world today. I think that the differences between Sunni and Shi'i would disappear in one instant. They are artificially maintained by the world in which we live. Do you agree?[11]

HA: Very definitely.

Question: Would you say that Imam Khomeini's stay in Paris will have a discernible impact on Muslims in Francophone Africa?

HA: I am not really in a position to say anything on that subject. All I know is that for the period of about ten days that I was in Paris I saw a large number of Muslims from different countries coming to visit Imam Khomeini. I do not recall seeing among them any Muslims from Francophone Africa. There were a large number from North Africa and Egypt coming not necessarily to talk to him but to pray behind him. I hear that there has been some influence of the revolution in Nigeria, that there has been an important echo of the revolution among the Muslims of Nigeria. Presumably the same will be the case in the Francophone countries, but whether as a result of his being in Paris, I do not know.

---

[11] In clarification of this remark, it might be said that the antagonisms arising from "the differences between Sunni and Shi'i" are indeed "artificially maintained," but that the differences themselves are deep-rooted and ultimately irreducible.

Question: Have other Muslim scholars, particularly Maulana Maudoodi, had any impact on the Imam Khomeini or vice versa? Has he had an influence on the well-known Muslim scholars and leaders of today?

HA: I do not know whether he has read any of the works of Maudoodi. This much is certain, that the message of support from Maudoodi to Imam Khomeini went in a very belated fashion in early January of this year, and Imam Khomeini expressed regret to me not merely that all the Muslim countries had refused him admission in a suitable fashion in October 1978, but that he had had not a single expression of effective support from the Islamic movement.

It is not likely, in the nature of things, that he should have concerned himself greatly with the works of Maudoodi. In a more general fashion, one could say that the Persian translation of some of the works of Maudoodi could have had an effect on people in Iran when circulated. Some may have had some effect, but who is to say how great is the effect? Whether Imam Khomeini has had an influence in the other direction upon Maudoodi or other Muslim leaders, I do not know. Unfortunately, there is no sign of it. Otherwise Maudoodi would hardly have accepted the King Faisal award for Islamic Studies.

Question: I know that you have done work on freemasonry in Iran and Turkey. Is there any evidence to suggest a link between the Shah and Zionism was forged through the medium of freemasonry?

HA: I think there were many channels of communication, linkages, overlapping interest, and so on. Probably freemasonry was one among them. In the aftermath of the revolution all the Masonic lodges have been closed in Iran and their entire archives have been captured intact. A preliminary selection of documents has already been published. They confirm what was suspected some time earlier. Many of the lodges in Tehran and elsewhere in

Iran were controlled by Jews or by Baha'is of Jewish origin, which furnishes another avenue of communication with Israel and Zionism generally. But one should not overestimate the importance of this one medium of communication when there were so many others available. Freemasonry played an important role on the domestic plane, but it is not necessarily connected with the question of Zionism.

Question: I want to return to the question of women. Being a Muslim one believes in community and that one is responsible for the community first. Have you ever come into contact with Kate Millett, who was sent out of Iran and who says she went there on a women's mission? What was her mission?

HA: I have had no communication with Kate Millett. I do not know what she thought her mission in Iran was. But irrespective of her, let me say a few words about the so-called women's demonstrations in Iran that took place for four or five days in succession. The alleged cause of the demonstrations was the curtailment of women's rights by the revolutionary regime. They coined a nice slogan for the occasion: "In the spring of freedom there is no freedom." Imam Khomeini, I think in the last public address that he gave before leaving Tehran to return to Qum, in a speech that touched on many subjects said "Now that we have in Iran an Islamic government, women should observe Islamic criteria of dress, particularly those that work in the ministries."

There are two things to be noticed. First, this was a recommendation. Secondly, it was directed particularly at women in government service. It was interpreted wilfully as a command to be enforced by coercive means if necessary and as meaning that all Iranian women must immediately cover themselves with the *chador*.[12] Seizing upon this recommendation in the speech of Imam Khomeini, a weird alliance of people organized a series of

---

[12] Subsequently the observance of *hijab* by Iranian women was, of course, enforced as a matter of law.

demonstrations in Tehran. Included among them were the leftists who, like most people who talk about equality, have a very elitist mentality. Seeing their lack of support among the working class in Iran, they have tried to seize upon a number of marginal issues and build them up as vehicles for their own attempts to gain power. One such vehicle was the women's demonstrations.

Those taking part in the demonstrations belonged primarily to the upper echelons of Tehran society. It was interesting to see television footage of those demonstrations. Many of the women were dressed in the latest fashions and had dyed their hair, which in the context is of significance. It shows a certain kind of self-hatred. It is the same kind of thing as one has seen in the United States, where Afro-Americans have tried to straighten out their hair. These were the people who were parading through the streets led by Kate Millett and calling for women's emancipation. Far larger demonstrations in support of Imam Khomeini and denunciation of these intrigues of the leftists on the one hand and the upper classes on the other went largely unreported in the western press. This was a bubble that burst very quickly.

THIRD LECTURE

Islam as Ideology: The thought of Ali Shari'ati

I shall speak today of the life, thoughts, and influence of the late Dr. Ali Shari'ati, whom one may briefly characterize as a major ideologue of the Islamic Revolution.

If the revolution in general has been led by the Shi'i *ulama*, primarily by Imam Khomeini, drawing on a long tradition, nonetheless it remains true that the work of Dr. Shari'ati also contributed to preparing a large number of the younger educated class in Iran to accept and follow with devotion and courage the leadership given by Imam Khomeini. Although Dr. Shari'ati in all his numerous writings hardly ever referred directly to the political, social and economic problems of contemporary Iran, and although his death in exile in England in July 1977 came before the revolution, he must be regarded as one of the major figures in the revolution.

Before examining the figure of Shari'ati, the content of his thought, and the nature of his influence, it may be useful to give some history of modern Islamic thought in Iran in the same way we gave a similar background for Imam Khomeini.

The background history of modern Islamic thought in Iran is relatively recent and can in no way compete with the centuries-old tradition of the Shi'i *ulama* as an institution and as a tradition in political leadership in Iran. In fact, we may say that one of the major reasons for the relative paucity of modern Islamic thinkers in Iran is precisely the leadership exercised by the Shi'i *ulama*. Whereas in other Islamic countries the *ulama* progressively lost their social and intellectual standing so that other individuals from outside the traditional institutions came forward to assume the task of reformulating Islam for the contemporary world, in Iran this was not the case.

As I have sought to demonstrate, the Shi'i *ulama* maintain their role in a fashion unparalleled anywhere else in the Muslim world. The near monopoly on the direction and expression of religious sentiment by the *ulama* tended naturally to militate against the emergence in Iran of figures who were also devoted to Islam but came from a different intellectual and social background than the *ulama*. It is for this reason that, for example, we do not see in Iran any figure such as Iqbal in the Indo-Pakistan subcontinent or any of the well-known modernist thinkers of the Arab world and Indonesia.

It is not until the postwar period that we see the beginning of a substantial development in Islamic thought and expression that is separate from the traditional concerns and institutions of the Shi'i *ulama*. This development comes in the aftermath of the expulsion of Reza Khan and the partial lifting of controls and repression by the now deposed Shah in the early years of his reign.

There arose at Tehran University an Islamic Students' Association that was by no means a simple student society but concerned itself with the propagation of Islam in the contemporary idiom. It was designed to attract the younger class, particularly those who had been subjected under Reza Khan to a secular education. Many of the figures, now well known worldwide because of their involvement in the revolution and the provisional government, had their first involvement in Islamic affairs precisely with this Islamic Students' Association at Tehran University, founded in 1942. For example, none other than Mehdi Bazargan, now prime minister of the provisional revolutionary government, but then a professor at the university was its chief patron. Even outside that organization, Bazargan must be regarded as the first and most important exponent of Islamic ideas in a modern fashion, before Dr. Shari'ati himself. As his title, Muhandis, indicates, Bazargan is an engineer by background and he enjoyed a scientific education abroad. At the same time, he was well grounded in Islamic subjects. Bringing together these two areas of concern and competence, he wrote a large number of books stressing a number of things.

The first was the complete congruence between Islam and the established findings of modern natural sciences, and the second was the applicability of Islam to contemporary social and political problems, together with the fact that Islam is a total way of life that addresses itself to all strata of the society. These ideas are put forward by him in a large number of books. To give one example of his method of thought, we may mention one of his books, entitled *Mutahhirat dar Islam*, on the prescriptions for ablution and cleansing in Islam, in which he demonstrates in great detail not merely the spiritual benefit but the hygienic and biological usefulness of all the provisions of Islam in this respect.

Bazargan was followed by a large number of other writers, who also each in his own way following approximately the same line of thought, came forward to write on Islamic subjects in a contemporary idiom designed to attract the allegiance of the secularly educated. Neither Bazargan nor any of the other figures that followed in his wake was able to exercise an influence comparable to that of the late Dr. Shari'ati, whom future historians of Iran may come to regard as one of the seminal figures in the prehistory of the Islamic Revolution. I think it is fair to say that once the full dimensions of his work become known he will be seen as one of the more important Muslim thinkers of the present century, in the range and impact of his thought comparable to the other names that are already familiar to Muslims.

Dr. Ali Shari'ati was born in 1933 in a village called Mazinan in the eastern part of Iran, in the desert region known as the Kavir. He was born into a family that for many generations had cultivated the religious sciences. In what is, in literary terms, one of his most accomplished books, he wrote a detailed memoir of his early background in the village and in particular of the great and formative influence exerted upon him by his father Muhammad Taqi Shari'ati.

At a fairly early age Dr. Shari'ati left with his father for Mashhad, where in 1946 his father established the Center for the Propagation of Islamic Truths (Kanun-i Nashr-i Haqa'iq-i Islami). 'Ali continued his education, first under the guidance of his father and then under that of the religious scholars in Mashhad, which after Qum is the second major center of religious learning in Iran.

At a very early age he showed an interest in going beyond the traditional. Building on the firm basis of learning and piety given to him by his father and other teachers, he continued to branch out in new directions and to gain new interests for himself. The first fruit of his interests was the translation from Arabic into Persian while he was still in his teens of a book on Abu Dharr al-Ghaffari by an Arab author, Jaudat as-Sahhar, in which the image is presented of Abu Dharr al-Ghaffari as a struggler against the perversions of the Islamic ideal that took place in the Umayyad period and a champion in the perpetual struggle of justice against injustice.

The interest in Abu Dharr al-Ghaffari on the part of Dr. Shari'ati was permanent throughout his life, and Abu Dharr al-Ghaffari became one of the archetypes of the Islamic perfect man, so to speak, and was frequently mentioned in Dr. Shari'ati's works.

Dr. Shari'ati then entered the newly founded teachers' training college in Mashhad to pursue his studies. Here also he did not restrict himself to the traditional. On the contrary, he read extremely widely and began to acquire a knowledge of French and other western languages, finishing at the top of his class. He was sent by the government for a period of study in France, which must be regarded as the second formative period in his life. He spent a total of five years in Paris, during which time he not only continued his formal studies in sociology but also established contact with a wide variety of intellectual and political circles. For example, he had close ties with leaders of the Algerian FLN, the National Liberation Front of Algeria in exile, and contributed articles to their French-language organ. Also in the context of his involvement with the leaders of the Algerian revolution, he made the acquaintance of the works of Frantz Fanon, the Martinique-born supporter of, and participant in, the Algerian revolution. He learned from Fanon the ideas of cultural alienation and psychological damage wrought by the excesses of imperialism. The interest he kindled in Fanon, still alive in Iran, resulted in the translation of his major works into Persian.

Beyond these contacts with the Algerian revolution, Dr. Shari'ati also had a wide range of contacts with other Arab and African anticolonialist strugglers and theoreticians in France. He formulated not merely a theoretical but also a practical interest in the problem of unity, unity of action as well as sentiment, between Iran and the rest of the Islamic world and beyond it with Africa and the Third World in general.

As for his purely intellectual and academic contacts, we may mention that while he was in France he also studied under, and made the personal acquaintance of, the French Orientalist, Louis Massignon, Jacques Berque and major theoreticians of contemporary European sociology such as Georges Gurvitch. He also engaged in a systematic study of Marxism, a study that is of great importance for two reasons. First, it was to enable him on a basis of knowledge and not mere hostility and fear to produce one of the most systematic and compelling critiques of Marxism to be written by a Muslim. Secondly, as with any debate or dialogue with an opponent, this debate and dialogue with Marxism left a certain imprint upon the work and thought of Dr. Shari'ati himself, not in the sense of absorbing any ideas of Marxism, which he thoroughly refuted, but merely in the sense of confronting certain problems at the forefront of Marxist dialectic in order to be able to refute them.[1]

---

[1] In point of fact, the influence of Marxism on Shari'ati did go somewhat deeper than indicated here; his predilection for binary oppositions as a means of analysing both history and society (see pp. 94-95) may fairly be linked to his critical interest in Marxism.

Apart from these multifarious contacts with Arab and African leaders in France and the world of French intellectual life, he was also heavily involved in Iranian exile politics. Before leaving Iran he had been briefly involved in the National Resistance Movement (Nahzat-i Muqavamat-i Milli), an organization which was fundamentally religious in its orientation, despite its title, and was the major organ of opposition to the Shah's regime after the American coup d'etat in August 1953. According to an erstwhile associate of Shari'ati, he also belonged to an oppositional group calling itself "the God-worshipping socialists" (*khudaparastan-i susialist*). The inclusion of the word *socialist* in the designation of the organization should be seen as evidence for the attraction exerted in Iran at the time by certain ideas of "Islamic socialism" current in the Arab world.

At the conclusion of his studies in France, he returned to Iran and immediately was arrested at the crossing point from Turkey. He was separated from his family without even being given the opportunity to see his father. This was in 1964. This first arrest of Dr. Shari'ati showed clearly that the regime had already recognized in him a dangerous opponent, not merely because of his political activity abroad, which was, after all, not uncommon among Iranian students whether in Europe or America, but because of the role of leadership that he had exerted and because of the intellectual dimension to his thought and activity, which by far transcended the normal agitation and concentration on demonstrations and shouting of slogans that was current among the Iranian opposition abroad.

After his release from prison some six months later, he was prevented from assuming any teaching position consonant with his abilities and qualifications. He was allowed only to act as a teacher in various high schools and later to teach courses in humanities at the College of Agriculture. After a time spent in this activity, whether by administrative mistake or for some other reason, he was able to gain a teaching post in the department of sociology at the University of Mashhad, where he swiftly acquired a huge following, so much so that his classes were attended not merely by the students of that department but by others from other parts of the university. This was because of the method that he followed in his teaching, which refused to restrict itself to the normal preoccupations of the academic life, which sought totally to discard once and for all the discredited notion of a value-free and uncommitted sociology. He made it plain from the very beginning that sociology, whether it acknowledges it or not, is the outcome of a certain worldview and certain loyalties and commitments, whether these are stated or not. He made it plain that his sociology was committed, that it drew its values from Islam, and had as its purpose the correct understanding of the contemporary reality of Iranian Islamic society and the change and reform of that society.[2]

It is not surprising, therefore, that pressure was soon exerted upon him compelling him to leave the university. But far from putting an end to his influence, this proved to be the prelude to the most influential and fruitful period of his life. Deprived of any formal academic appointment, he began giving a vast number of lectures in various institutions across the country. He was invited constantly by students at various colleges and universities throughout Iran. Most important of all, he concentrated his activity at an institution of religious propagation in Tehran known as the Husayniya-yi Irshad. The first part of this designation refers to an institution or place in which the sufferings and martyrdom of Imam Husayn are related for pious commemoration. This activity might have a primarily emotional purpose, but the addition of the word *Irshad* ("guidance") to the name of the Tehran institution made plain that its function was not merely emotional gratification and the shedding of tears once a year during Muharram. On the contrary, it aimed at a more active and purposeful form of guidance towards change in the affairs of society.

---

2 It is worth noting that despite the fame he acquired as a sociologist of a unique and original type, Shari'ati's doctoral work in Paris was in Iranian philology, not sociology.

Dr. Shari'ati's major lectures were given at this institution. Here again he attracted huge audiences when he put forward all the distinctive themes of his philosophy and outlook, which I shall attempt to recapitulate. He also toured constantly throughout the country giving lectures. The texts of numerous of these lectures, though not all, were recorded and transcribed and circulated in book form.

Such was the reception given to the teaching and lectures of Dr. Shari'ati that the Husayniya-yi Irshad was closed down in 1973 and he was imprisoned again this time for two years, and subjected to the abuse and torture that were common under the Pahlavi regime for all political prisoners. After an additional two years of internal banishment, he was released on the understanding that he would go into exile. Before he went abroad the Iranian regime tried to discredit him by one of the subtle tricks that it frequently employed. Shortly after his release, without his knowledge or permission, they published in one of the major Tehran daily newspapers in the form of a series of articles his critique of Marxism, which has been translated into English under the title *Marxism and other Western Fallacies — An Islamic Critique*.[3] Although the text of these lectures was more or less accurate, the circumstances of their publication were obviously intended by the government to imply that he had agreed to collaborate with the regime as a condition of his release. Indeed, such undertakings were given by a number of other opposition figures under varying degrees of duress, so that after their release they either kept silent or collaborated with the regime. By publishing these articles, the regime hoped to give the impression that Dr. Shari'ati had done the same.

Dr. Shari'ati protested and sought legal assistance, but to no avail. He was then obliged to go into exile, leaving behind his immediate family in the hope that they would join him soon after. He came to England and died in England in July 1977, apparently of a heart attack. Suspicions of assassination by the Iranian security police immediately arose. I believe that the coroner's report

---

[3] Translated by R. Campbell and published by Mizan Press of Berkeley, California, in 1980.

issued at the time made no mention of unnatural causes, but the suddenness of Shari'ati's death caused inevitable doubts and suspicions. Moreover, we know that one of the sons of Imam Khomeini, Mustafa, also died in a sudden and mysterious fashion in a way that also suggests involvement by the Iranian security police. Even if it not be a question of poisoning or some other fashion of assassination, in the sense that Ali Shari'ati had suffered continually at the hands of the Iranian security police and had been sent by them into exile, dying there, he may be thought to deserve the title of martyr that people in Iran have bestowed upon him.

I now turn to some of the major themes of his work. If we were to try to summarize the achievement of Dr. Shari'ati in one sentence it would be to say that he presented Islam not as a religion in the sense commonly understood by western usage, that is, a spiritual and moral matter concerning only or primarily the relations of the individual with his Creator -- but rather as an ideology -- that is, a comprehensive view of the world and reality and a plan for the full realization of human potential, individually and collectively, in such a way as to fulfill the whole purpose of man's being. When we try to describe Islam as anything else in terms of any of the categories of western thought and language, the result will inevitably be imperfect. It may be objected that in the same way as "religion" is inadequate to describe the reality of Islam, so too is "ideology," since it implies a system of ideas, and ideas by definition may be correct or may not be correct. Islam, at least for us Muslims, is something concerning the correctness and veracity of which there can be no doubt. So when Shari'ati applies the word *ideology* to his presentation of Islam it is not to imply that Islam is an ideology in the commonly understood sense. What is intended is a comprehensiveness, a totality, that does not restrict itself merely to a moral purification of the individual and the establishment of a spiritual link between the individual and God. I think this is what can be concluded from Shari'ati's use of the word *ideology*.

The foundation of Dr Shari'ati's scheme of ideas is what he calls the worldview, of *tawhid*, oneness. He has his own interpretation and presentation of the doctrine of *tawhid*. He stresses that, as he puts it, reality is one, not in the sense of the *wahdat al-wujud* of the Sufis, but rather in the sense that the spiritual and the material, this world and the hereafter, constitute a single continuum for the Muslim, and when he is confronted with them he makes no distinction between them. He sees himself not as a stranger in nature, something apart from it, but rather as being, together with nature, of a single origin and single purpose. This living unity of the entirety of reality, of man and the universe, is a reality that has a certain purpose as well as unity, and a certain direction, a direction of the attainment of ever growing perfection.

This is the fundamental, *tawhid*. Built on it, or deriving from it, are three major branches of the ideas of Dr. Shari'ati. The first is sociology. Here we mean his own concept, not any of the imported schools of sociology, Marxist or otherwise. He means by sociology a view of the nature of society and even the terminology for the discussion of society that are drawn from the Qur'an and the other sources of Islam. He asserts that there are two fundamental forms of society in existence, both in the contemporary world and in the past. There is the society based upon *shirk*, upon the assignment of partners to Allah; and there is the society based upon *tawhid*, which has its separate characteristics. For him this is the fundamental cleavage, not capitalist and communist, or democratic and dictatorial.

Then there is anthropology, by which we do not mean in this context the study of societies, of distinct, particularly primitive societies -- the recording and analysis of their various habits, mores, and customs. We mean a coherent view and teaching concerning the nature of man and his reality. Dr. Shari'ati in numerous works returns to this theme: What is man and what is the essential nature of man? He says that man is essentially a being that has two poles -- the lowly substance of clay from which, according to the Qur'an, he was created; and the spirit of God, which has been infused in him as the life-giving principle. Man is not a static being. On the contrary, he is a continuous and inevitable process of becoming, away from the lowly principle or pole of clay towards the sublime principle of the spirit of God contained within him.

Next comes the philosophy of history, which is also based upon Shari'ati's reading of the Qur'an and which sees the entirety of history as a conflict of forces. In the same way that man himself is the battleground for the competing forces of his lowly origin, his lowly bodily nature, and the element of divine spirit contained within him, history is also a battleground where *tawhid* and *shirk*, justice and injustice, have continually opposed each other. Here he makes a particular reference to an episode that is touched upon only lightly in the Qur'an -- that of the fratricide of Cain and Abel. In this he sees the archetype for the continuous struggle throughout history between two different types of man, two different types of society, two different types of worldview.

It can be said that these subjects -- sociology, anthropology, philosophy, and history -- are particular derivations or applications of the general worldview of *tawhid*. They in turn form an ideology that is a comprehensive programme for action, which in turn has as its purpose the construction of an ideal society -- and that in turn an ideal man.

The term given by Dr. Shari'ati to the ideal society is none other than the familiar Islamic term of *ummah*, the etymology of which he analyzes, coming to the conclusion that an *ummah* is a society based upon no particular organizing principle of race or class, but united only by the pursuit of a certain goal and moving towards it under the correct form of leadership. Here also ties in his understanding of the word *imam*, which has a certain distinct meaning in the Shi'i context but is given an additional meaning by Dr. Shari'ati as the leader of a self-conscious, aware society, which has chosen a certain direction for itself and is moving towards it. From this ideal society of the *ummah* will emerge also the ideal man.

Of course, there is much more to be said about each of these components of the thought system of Dr. Shari'ati, but I think this will give you an idea of the major themes of his thought. In addition to this kind of systematic presentation of Islam in a manner and idiom that were able to secure the loyalty to Islam of large numbers of young, educated people in Iran who had been alienated by secularism and materialism, there are one or two other dimensions of his thought that I would like to bring out.

I turn first to his view of the Shi'i school of thought in Islam. Dr. Shari'ati subjected to a critical revision many of the major concepts of the Shi'i school. I have already alluded to the particular meaning he gave to the word *imam* as applied to the Twelve Imams of the Ah' al-Bayt. He says at one point in his works that for Shi'i Muslims, the *imam* has become a sanctified, semi-divine being, in memory of whom they shed tears and at the very mention of whom they begin to tremble, but who has no influence on the actual conduct and direction of their lives.

He reinterpreted the notion of waiting for the reemergence of the Twelfth Imam, which might be taken as the pretext for a mere passive stance of idleness and inactivity. He taught that waiting for the Imam essentially meant anticipating the circumstances of his return, trying to pave the way for it by bringing about a just and pious society.

Also important in Dr. Shari'ati's view of Shi'i school was his attempt to interpret it in such a way as not to exaggerate and enlarge the inevitable differences between Shi'i and Sunni Muslims. In a very interesting book entitled *Safavi Shi'ism and Alavi Shi'ism,* he criticized the coercive methods used by the Safavids for the imposition of a particular form of Shi'i thought on Iran and sought to discard the cultural forms Iranian Shi'ism had acquired in the Safavid period. It may be as well to explain briefly the sense of this title, by which he meant that there was a certain form of "establishment" Shi'ism promoted by monarchy, the Safavi monarchy, that was a distortion. It expressed itself in violence against Sunnis and violated the very spirit of Shi'i thought by implicitly legitimizing monarchy. On the other hand, opposed to Safavi Shi'ism is Alavi Shi'ism, original and authentic Shi'ism of Imam 'Ali (upon whom be peace) the Shi'ism that exists eternally in contrast and in opposition to Safavi Shi'ism.

Because of these distinctive views of Shi'i thought and its history, Dr. Shari'ati was accused by certain people of being a crypto-Sunni or even a Wahhabi. It should be pointed out that although he received overwhelming acclaim from the young generation in Iran, other segments of religious opinion held a more negative view of him.

In connection with this, we should also mention one other constant theme of Dr. Shari'ati's work, which is best summed up in the title of one of his books, *Mazhab 'Alayhi Mazhab* (*Religion Against Religion*). In the book and elsewhere he said that religion as a historical phenomenon has two distinct ways of appearing. It may become either an instrument in the hands of the ruling class, the established interests of corruption and distortion, as one of the means at their disposal for the control and exploitation of that society; or a means of struggle for the realization of truth and the establishment of a just society.

In a very interesting insight he points out that all the prophets descended from Abraham mentioned in the Qur'an, as well as Abraham himself find the beginning of their historical career in opposition to the existing secular order. This was so with Abraham; Moses; Jesus and Muhammad himself (peace be upon all of them). This is for Shari'ati an indication of the essential nature and purpose of religion -- not merely to propound a message of salvation in the hereafter but also to throw down a challenge to existing secular authority and take hold of the existing social, economic, and political reality of man and transform it into a shape acceptable to God, conforming with man's purpose.

I have already gone over my time, but there is one matter I would like to touch on before concluding. There has recently appeared in Iran a terrorist organization by the name of Furqan, which has carried out two assassinations, that of the first Chief of the General Staff of the Islamic Republic, Major General Qarani; and that of Ayatullah Murtaza Mutahhari, one of the members of the Council of the Revolution. In the communiques published by

Furqan they claim to be following the thought of the late Dr. Shari'ati. They claim to be preaching a revolutionary mode of Islam opposed to the *akhunds*.[4]

It has been credibly asserted in Iran that this Furqan group is transparently a creation of the CIA and of the United States, which has realized the importance of Dr. Shari'ati and the legacy of his thought in Iran and is seeking to create division in the Islamic camp by dividing the people into the followers of Shari'ati and the followers of Imam Khomeini and the rest of the *ulama* aligned with him.

There are a number of pieces of evidence in this respect to which I have personally had access. For example, when the new American ambassador was nominated, a number of academics were invited to brief him on topics of interest. I was invited to brief him precisely on the subject of Dr. Shari'ati, his thought and influence.[5] It is very interesting that on the same day another academic was invited to give a lecture on the problem of ethnic minorities in Iran, which is also a topic of considerable significance given the current attempts at destabilization in Iran.

It is also reported that the CIA has engaged a certain lady to prepare a complete English translation of Dr. Shariati's works for internal consumption.

In any event, this attempt is no doubt doomed to failure, since the vast majority of young Iranians in particular who support the Islamic Revolution in that country are simultaneously the followers of Imam Khomeini and Dr. Shari'ati. There is no question of a choice or contradiction facing them. It can be said that Imam Khomeini has supplied in a masterful fashion the strategic and political leadership, as well as much of the spiritual inspiration.

---

4 *Akhund*, originally an honorific bestowed on scholars of exceptional erudion, later became a pejorative implying contempt for the whole class of ulama (when used by secularists) or for the ignorant and corrupt among them (when used by religious scholars themselves, including on occasion Imam Khomeini himself).

5 I did not accept the invitation.

Dr. Shari'ati, by contrast, has supplied and may continue to supply, even posthumously, the intellectual content for their commitment to the Revolution.[6]

---

[6] It is true that in the short term no contradiction was experienced by young Iranians who were "simultaneously the followers of Imam Khomeini and Dr. Shari'ati." Not long after the revolution, however, conflict did arise between those who regarded themselves as the heirs to Shari'ati's thought (the "religious intellectuals" [*raushanfikran-i mazhabi*], to use their own self-designation), and the *'ulama* who were presiding over the nascent Islamic Republic. This conflict became encapsulated in the slogan of "authentic Islam" (*Islam-i maktabi*) versus "syncretic Islam" (*Islam-i iltiqati*), the latter referring largely although not exclusively to the ideas of Shari'ati. A certain amount of polemical literature for and against Shari'ati was published in the mid-1980's. It was largely these controversies surrounding his ideas - especially the tendency to assert a leadership role for the intellectuals instead of the religious scholars (or at best together with them) - that led to a gradual diminution of his posthumous influence. At the same time, however, his ideas began to appear dated at the latest by the beginning of the 1990's: the constant references to Sartre, Camus, and Fanon no longer appeared daring or fresh, and the cultural climate and socio-political reality of Iran had changed beyond recognition from the years in which Shari'ati was lecturing and writing. His writings now appear to be of chiefly historical interest, illustrating a tendency that was important in preparing the way for the revolution. Shari'ati himself might fairly be designated as a transitional figure between the pre-revolutionary and revolutionary periods.

DISCUSSION

Question: The speaker is no doubt aware of the promise concerning the coming of Imam Mahdi. How does this fit in with Shi'i belief and might Imam Khomeini be Imam Mahdi?

HA: There are number of qualifications set out in the appropriate sources and in tradition for the qualifications of the Mahdi. Imam Khomeini does not fulfill them. I do not think that anyone except SAVAK agents during the course of the Revolution sought to create any confusion on this point. Nobody else suggested that Imam Khomeini might be the Mahdi. At one point certain SAVAK agents put a rumor around to create confusion and disturbance, but nothing came of it.

I think that I outlined the concept of Mahdi briefly in my first lecture, that Shi'i Muslims believe in a succession of twelve imams, the last of whom -- Imam Muhammad al Mahdi -- disappeared from the physical plane in 874 C. E. in the city of Samarra in northern Iraq, and that he will ultimately reemerge in Mecca (may his reappearance he hastened). As for the various signs that will indicate his coming, these are to a large extent identical with the signs that we find in Sunni sources for the coming of the Mahdi. The Sunni belief is that the Mahdi will have a normal life span, without occultation, and that he will appear in either Syria or Khorasan. But other general descriptions, eschatological descriptions, of the last days that will precede his coming, are common to both Shi'i and Sunni sources. I do not think that one can say anything useful about how the present situation in Iran relates. Whether you take it as a sign that the return of the Mahdi is near, I do not know. I know of no useful way of approaching that question.[7]

---

[7] It is, however, significant that the triumph of the revolution occasioned a heightened interest in the theme of the Twelfth Imam and his anticipated return; enough books were published on the subject for a special exhibition to be organized in Tehran, which I had the occasion to visit in December 1979. In addition,

Question: My question concerns what we call in Arabic *tarbiya* ("training") which many workers in the Islamic movement consider one basic concept to prepare for change, to bring back Islam and build, or rebuild, a state of Islam. We gather that the Pahlavis worked hard to uproot all the Islamic principles in Iran. Therefore, until recently there was no chance for Islamic activities to flourish and lead to such *tarbiya*. When the Revolution took place, was there a chance to work out this *tarbiya*? To someone like me who is not aware of exactly what is going on, it seems that there is a sort of layer on the surface formed by the development of events, but that the message did not go deeply into the heart of the Muslim individual in Iran.

That is reflected when we gather that there is a front forming the political entity that governs Iran. This front is composed of people who belong to Imam Khomeini, the Islamic Liberation Movement of Mr. Bazargan, and other factions. Do you see this scenario as a point of weakness? What is the role of *tarbiya*, and what was done towards it in order to strengthen the solidarity of Muslims in Iran, to protect the revolution and keep it up until it achieves its ultimate goals?

HA: You raised two points -- the depth, or lack of it, of the Islamic commitment of the majority of people and the problem of disunity or division within the Islamic camp. One should not doubt a great depth of commitment by the overwhelming masses of the Iranian people. Indeed, without this commitment it would hardly have been possible for the revolution to take place. Since the revolution triumphed in the face of overwhelming odds, a commitment that was less than profound or less than complete could not possibly have succeeded in the face of the great alliance of power and coercion that was ranged against it. We should not con-

---

the slogan chanted on various occasions throughout the last ten years of Imam Khomeini's life - "O God, preserve Khomeini until the revolution of the Mahdi" -- expressed clearly the belief that the Islamic Revolution of Iran constituted a species of active preparation for the relatively imminent return of the Twelfth Imam.

fuse depth of commitment with depth of knowledge. These are different things, although it is hoped the depth of commitment will lead to the depth of knowledge.

One point that I might have made about the influence of Dr. Shari'ati is that there is a certain danger among some young Iranians that they have made their acquaintance with Islam exclusively through his works and tend to understand Islam only by this channel and to develop a certain narrowness of mind and attitude, something that the late Dr. Shari'ati presumably never intended. He made it very plain that he intended to stimulate thought, not to lay down in a dogmatic fashion a certain number of doctrines for people to accept without question. In the case of a number of young Iranians whose acquaintance with Islam is recent and only by way of his works there are some problems of knowledge and understanding Islam. This is not restricted in any way to Iran and Dr Shari'ati. In the Arab world we see people who will read only the books of Sayyid Qutb as if those exhausted all need for understanding and study. We see in Pakistan people who read only the works of Maudoodi, as though they were the last word on everything. It is a general tendency among contemporary Muslims.

Given this reservation, we can say that there is certainly a very deep emotional commitment to Islam, which needs supplementing by a more profound and broader knowledge of Islam. It was often said in the western press during the Revolution that it was a kind of loose coalition of different forces -- the secularists, leftists, and Muslims, but this was never really true. All that was ever asked for by the secularists, people who are today coming together in various groups and parties, was the implementation of the existing constitution and maybe a few reforms here and there. But the revolution, as opposed to the demand for a few reforms and adjustments and human rights, was exclusively the work of the Muslim masses in Iran. At no point was there a question of coalition. The masses are still there in Iran. Just a few days ago there was a vast demonstration in Tehran in condemnation of the various foreign intrigues against the Revolution as well as their local agents.

I do not think you can speak of any serious division in the Islamic camp. There are certainly differences of opinion between Imam Khomeini and the government of Mehdi Bazargan on certain points. There are differences of opinion, approach, and outlook between Imam Khomeini and Ayatullah Shari'atmadari. But I think it is a mistake to expect a sort of dictatorial, monolithic unity. The existence of these differences, on condition they are not pushed to the point of division, capable of exploitation by the foreign enemies of the Revolution, may even be regarded as positive.

Every crisis in Iran since the Revolution has been heralded with great glee by the western press as the beginning of the downfall of the Islamic Republic of Iran. There was a certain incident a few months ago when the sons of Ayatullah Taleqani were arrested in Tehran for a few days. I was then contacted by the representative of one of the television networks in America and invited to participate in a programme on the upcoming civil war in Iran. I asked him what civil war he had in mind, and he replied, "Between the followers of Ayatullah Khomeini on the one hand and the followers of Ayatullah Taleqani on the other." I said, "We'll let the civil war begin and then we'll see." The matter was settled in a fairly peaceful way in just two or three days.

When you look at the reports of unrest and trouble, what is called anarchy and chaos, do not underestimate the problems in Iran, which are natural and inevitable, but also do not get excessively upset and think that things will fall apart. I find it particularly curious that the American press always speaks of anarchy and chaos in Iran in a country where personal safety in the streets of the capital cannot be guaranteed.

Comment: I was interested in your observation that Dr. Shari'ati had been labeled a crypto-Sunni or crypto-Wahhabi, but in fact his exposition of the *tawhid* doctrine looks very much as if it would suggest that he is a crypto-Sufi. I find it difficult to distinguish this from the orthodox sufi view.

HA: I would tend to agree. I think that Dr. Shari'ati's main strength lay in his exposition of sociology. When it came to matters of metaphysics, I think he had a rather weaker grasp. Since he never made fully plain what he understood to be the Sufi view, it is difficult to see where the difference lies between his own understanding of *tawhid* and the Sufi understanding.

Also, from many of his works it becomes apparent that he understands Sufism to be equivalent to Hallaj, whereas Hallaj is by no means a typical representative of Sufi tradition. The fact that Dr. Shari'ati regarded him as such is due, I think, to the influence of Professor Louis Massignon, who had a personal, inward involvement with Hallaj for reasons of his own and sought to promote him as a typical representative of Islamic spirituality, whereas in fact he was not.

When we assess Dr. Shari'ati's work, there are two things to be said. First, he died at a relatively early age before he had had the chance to complete the task of forming a mature and fully coherent school of thought. Secondly, his works that remain are, with few exceptions, the transcribed texts of lectures. It is not as if he had the leisure to sit down at his writing desk and think carefully over every word that he committed to paper. It is largely a question of lectures, which were recorded, transcribed, and printed in most cases without his having the opportunity even to revise and proofread them. There is therefore a certain uneven quality about many of the published texts, which characterizes all lectures -- including the one being given today!

Dr Kalim Siddiqui: You said in the introduction to Ali Shari'ati's book *On the Sociology of Islam* that he was conscious that his would be a short life, that somehow he was conscious of imminent death. Why was this so?

HA: I think this was a reasonable conclusion to be drawn from the nature of his activity, the context in which he exercised it, and the fact that any opponent of the regime in Iran had to reckon with imprisonment or sudden death or martyrdom. I do not think we should look for any obscure cause. It was simply a reasonable inference from the conditions of Iran under the Pahlavi regime.

Question: You spoke in your lecture about the tension between Shari'ati and some of the traditional *ulama*. Could you throw more light on that? Does the problem stem from the fact that Shari'ati moved backwards, as it were, from sociology into Islam, rather than stemming from a religious background, by which I mean religious learning?

HA: That is a reasonable assessment. Although the entire content of his writing is religious, the style, the manner of formulation, is obviously not traditional, and we can state without any qualms, owes a great deal to his western education and his encounter with, and refutation of, Marxism. Shari'ati was a man who without embarrassment would speak of Marx, Nietzsche, Fanon and a large number of other strange and unfamiliar-sounding names, which would arouse repugnance in certain traditionalist circles in Iran.

Some adherents of Shari'ati have suggested that there were certain personal elements involved. Crucial, however, were general differences of outlook and specific points of disagreement, such as the evaluation of Mulla Muhammad Baqir Majlisi, the great scholar of the late Safavid period.

In the book that I have already mentioned, *Safavi Shi'ism and Alavi Shi'ism*, Dr. Shari'ati attacks Majlisi as a prime representative of what he calls Safavi Shi'ism, which in his view is a distortion of true Shi'ism. But from a more traditional point of view, it cannot be overlooked that among his other accomplishments Majlisi is the compiler of the *Bihar al-Anwar*, the huge compendium of Shi'i tradition. He is also the author of a large number of other works, that continue in use in Iran down to the present day.

Ayatullah Mutahhari, a close associate of Imam Khomeini, was among those who differed with Shari'ati on this and associated topics, and his disquiet was conveyed to the Imam at his place of exile in Najaf. Later, when the Imam had returned to Iran, a friend of mine who was an admirer of Shari'ati went to the Imam in part in order to seek his opinion of Shari'ati. He asked first what in his estimation were the major causes of the revolution and its success, to which the Imam responded that Allah had willed it, and that His will had manifested itself in such and such ways. He then asked: "Do you not think that the work of the late Dr. Shari'ati also was of great effect?" To this the Imam replied, simply and factually, that Shari'ati's teachings had aroused controversy and discussion among the *ulama* but at the same time played a role in orienting younger intellectuals to Islam. He also said that the followers of Shari'ati should go beyond what he had offered them to investigate the formal religious sciences.

One thing that I should have pointed out with respect to the influence of Dr. Shari'ati is that he has also had an influence on some of the younger *ulama*. It was interesting when listening to some of the tape recordings of the *khutbas* given in Iran during the Revolution to find constant echos in them of the ideas and even the terms of Dr. Shari'ati. So he also had a great influence there.

Question: I very well understand the classification of knowledge presented by Dr. Shari'ati, but to me it seems a little too abstract. Can you elaborate?

HA: Ideas by their nature are abstract, and I am not sure how I can make them less abstract. Obviously his scheme of things claims no final authority for itself. One is under no obligation to accept it. It is simply the statement of certain themes of Islam in a coherent form. It may be oversimplified, but it is nonetheless of some utility in that it shows the basis of all things in Islam to be *tawhid* and the ultimate application of *tawhid* through these various ways to be the creation of an ideal man, who has fully realized the purpose for which he has been created.

I do not think we need be so narrowly *salafi* and ask, "Where did you get this from? Where is it in Qur'an and hadith?" The elements of it are present in Qur'an and hadith. It is simply that they have been put together in a certain pattern. Those who find it useful are free to accept it, and those who do not are welcome not to. Nobody has any argument with it.

Dr. Kalim Siddiqui: Would you agree that a certain climate of opinion has to be created in a situation like that in Iran under the Pahlavi dynasty before such a revolution can occur, and that this is what Dr. Shari'ati succeeded in doing? Much of the work that we intellectuals do is attacked by the practical men of this world as being "pie in the sky", not very relevant, and so on. They say, "Let's get down to the ground and do some work instead of talking and writing about it." Does the work of Dr. Ali Shari'ati in any way vindicate our work, or are we still the useless people?

HA: It is interesting that precisely this point is made by Dr. Shari'ati in the first of the extracts translated in the book *On the Sociology of Islam*. He says there that some people say we have been talking and writing long enough, and it is time to get down to action. He says that on the contrary we have not yet talked or written adequately from a proper perspective. This dichotomy of either thinking and planning or acting is in itself a false dichotomy as the two are interrelated and proceed together.

Comment: The feeling of disquiet between Ayatullah Mutahhari and Dr. Shari'ati, that you referred to was perhaps psychological, but the reasons go much deeper. I had direct contact with the late Ayatullah Mutahhari who confided to me a number of points. He questioned all the basic concepts that Shari'ati put forward and introduced into our culture -- his philosophy, the very notion of *tawhid* according to his explanation. Ayatullah Mutahhari thought that Sharia'ati was an instrumentalist, in the sense that he used religion as an instrument for his political and social objectives. I am not saying that here we are dealing with his beliefs, inside his heart, but objectively, in his lectures and books. That was the sort of thing that gave this impression to the *ulama*, and that was the main reason for the tension between Ayatullah Mutahhari and him. It was not only Ayatullah Mutahhari who disagreed with him. There were many others, including Imam Khomeini himself. They covered a wide range.[8]

Dr Kalim Siddiqui: Could it be that the language of Ali Shari'ati was not understood in its entirety by the traditional sector in Iran because he represented the modern, western-educated sector, and that the coming together was the basic cause, rather than the concepts involved?

HA: It would be nice to say that it was only a question of language and formulation, but I do not think so. I think that the comment just made by the brother is right. I did not mean to imply that it was a question of personal jealousy between the two people. Of course, there were far more substantial issues. It is a question not only of formulation but of content. In my lecture I did not necessarily mean that whatever Dr. Shari'ati has said is the last word on any subject. This is not a claim that he made for himself. He always said that Islam was a becoming; not being in a static sense but evolution. He applied this concept to his own thought.

I have not read such a huge amount of his works, but I have read all his major works, the entirety of *Islam shinasi*, etc. However one views the doctrinal acceptability of his views, there is a undeniably certain stimulating quality in his writings, a mind at work, which is a thing all too rare in the Muslim world. There is a mind at work that is not intimidated by the West in any of its dimensions in order to resort to polemics and apologetics. It is engaged in an experiment, a rediscovery, a reformulation of a certain tradition. As a collective body, the *ulama*, despite their importance, which I have emphasized, have not been able to do this. Maybe it has not been their task. Dr. Shari'ati has been able to achieve something that they have not. It is not enough to issue *fatvas* to lead a whole generation back to Islam.

What was the difference between 1963 and the Revolution? What took place in those fifteen years? Why did the Shah leave in

---

[8] I now share this estimate.

the space of only a few days, when he could crush an uprising in 1963? Why was he compelled to leave the country in 1978? It is because a certain process took place in those years within Iran that supplemented the continuing activities of Imam Khomeini outside the country.

It seems to me that the most clearly identifiable internal factor in this process of preparation for revolution was the work of Dr. Shari'ati. Whatever one may think of this or that statement or doctrine of Dr. Shari'ati, his achievement that cannot be denied is that he led back a large part of the alienated middle class youth to an identification with Islam. Maybe their understanding of Islam needs refining, and in some cases correcting, but the commitment is there, and in many cases it is the single-handed work of Dr. Shari'ati. This is an achievement that one's disagreement with this or that point of his writings cannot efface.

Comment: You said that you should capture the weapons of the enemy and fight with them. That is precisely what Ali Shari'ati did when he moved to France, by forming the Group of God-Fearing Socialists. It puzzles me that a person like him had to invent this term. In your opinion, was it the people who were God-fearing or the people who were socialists, who were exploited by the invention of this term? Was he not in the beginning more influenced by socialism, then changing to God-fearing, the group then becoming a freedom movement?

HA: I think you misunderstood what I said. First, the group was not his creation. He was a member of it in Iran before going to Paris for his studies. Neither the group nor the term was his creation; he was merely a member, as were a number of other people.

As for the whole question of Islamic socialism, about which so many pages have been blackened and so much ink has been spilt, of course it is objectionable to take socialism as the basis and then use Islam as a qualifier. There is no doubt about that. But there are a number of things to be said.

First, at a certain time there was a currency in the Arab world of these ideas, and not only on the part of the Nasser regime in Egypt. There was also Mustafa Sibai, in Syria, writing a book called *Ishtirakiyat al-Islam* (*Socialism of Islam*), which created a considerable echo and impact. There is the simple human phenomenon that whoever is the enemy of your enemy you will regard as your friend. Therefore, a number of Iranians, seeing this kind of shadow enmity between various Arab regimes, particularly Egypt, and the Shah, tended to look upon intellectual developments in the Arab world, including Egypt, with some favor. This, I think, applies to the origin of this partial, passing interest in the idea of socialism.

Looking at the works of Dr. Shari'ati, including the critique of Marxism, you will see a thorough and clear refutation of socialism by him. It is not that he was a one-time socialist who became a Muslim or sought to achieve an incoherent mixture of the two. That is not the case.

It is true that we have a doctrine of Islamic socialism that has been formulated and has been criticized, but on the other hand we have a practice of Islamic capitalism. Nobody has formulated the theory of it, but the ugly reality of it is there. I do not know whether any of our *ulama* have given *fatvas* against Islamic capitalism, even though it is far more of an ugly reality in the Islamic world than so-called Islamic socialism.

Comment: To return to Dr. Shari'ati's role during the formative period of the Revolution, it seems to me that, as we have already discussed, there is a certain anticlerical, if not an anti-*ulama*, stance in his work. It seems to me that Mutahhari, as perhaps one of the best philosophers to emerge from contemporary Iran, had this at the back of his mind when he disagreed with the philosophical basis of Dr. Shari'ati's work. Indeed, about five years ago when I was reflecting on the situation in Iran, it seemed to me that the work of Dr. Shari'ati had formed a basis on the one hand for stimulating intellectuals to Islam but also on the other hand for stimulating it in a direction that would alienate them from the established *ulama*. This was the danger, I think, posed by people like Mehdi Bazargan and Shari'ati to a greater extent.

HA: I think it is an oversimplification to describe the late Dr. Shari'ati as anticlerical or anti-*ulama* as such. He criticizes certain aspects of the traditional religious establishment in Iran, and many of those criticisms may be justified.[9] But to say that he consistently opposes the institution of the *ulama* as such is a different matter. I do not think this can be documented from his works. In fact, he makes a clear distinction between the true *alim* and what he calls the mere *mu'ammam*, somebody who wears the turban and cloak without necessarily having the appropriate religious knowledge and commitment. But he makes it very clear that he is full of respect for the genuine *alim*.

As to whether what Mutahhari feared would take place, that the people under the influence of Shari'ati would not prove amenable to *ulama* leadership, I do not know. But certainly what has happened is not that. On the contrary, as I have already said, many people were ready to participate in the Revolution under the leadership of Imam Khomeini to a certain degree because of the influence upon them of Dr. Shari'ati.

There are problems in the relationship, as the other brother pointed out. There is no absolute harmony. There is not a neat dovetailing of the *ulama* and the influence of Shari'ati, but in general terms they have complemented each other.

Because there is a problem there, the foreign enemies of the Revolution -- primarily the United States -- have sought to inflate this and create a real problem, creating a camp of what they call followers of Shari'ati, Shari'atists so to speak, on the one hand and Khomeinists on the other. These terms are actually used in the American press. Anyone with the least acquaintance with young Iranians both inside and outside the country who form one of the

---

9 It is worth mentioning in passing that both before and after the revolution Imam Khomeini himself frequently criticised the excessive conservatism and intellectual stagnation of some of the 'ulama, without, of course, the mention of any names.

major elements of the Revolution knows that they are at the same time followers of Imam Khomeini and the enthusiastic students of Dr. Shari'ati. They do not perceive any contradiction. On the philosophical, purely intellectual plane there are problems and contradictions, but when it comes to political and social effect I would say that there are no major problems.[10]

Dr Kalim Siddiqui: May I take up the point about Islamic socialism and capitalism? I entirely agree with your stricture, with this exception. I believe that although the expression "Islamic capitalism" is not used, much of Islamic capitalism goes under the name of Islamic economics. There is a vast literature called Islamic economics and a large number of Islamic economists are being bred in Middle Eastern universities, changing their name from Muslim to Islamicists. These kinds of semantics are being developed and used. This is all within the framework of Islamic capitalism. I would go a stage further and say Islamic imperialism as well. It is not just developed. It is being practiced and institutionalized.

HA: I agree.

Question: What happened in the Arab world is that prior to Mustafa Sibai's book we had Sayyid Qutb's work in Egypt dealing with the same subject. But here I find it is quite a different thing, and I do not know how you evaluate it. Sibai and Sayyid Qutb were people of a religious background to start with, and then they went to tackle the matter of economics and so on, while Dr. Shari'ati was closer to sociology and economics and then moved to religious subjects.

As you said in your discussion, it is unacceptable to have socialism as the foundation and then you try to fit Islam with it. But the other way round could be acceptable, that Islam is the basis and then you tackle any modern situation. We can derive from it, so that always the derivation will be based on certain measures that are acceptable to Muslims.

---

[10] See n. 6 on p. 99.

What line would you suggest should be followed -- that we start with Qur'an and *sunnah* and then tackle the other subjects, or that we start basically from the so-called secular sciences and then there is no need to go very deep into the real sources?

HA: We do Dr. Shari'ati injustice if we suppose that he began from a secular background and then started studying Qur'an and so on. That is not so. He grew up in a thoroughly Islamic household, and his father, a man learned in religion, was the earliest formative influence on his life. It is not a question of his later acquiring Islamic knowledge in a superficial and haphazard way, in such a way that the dominant element in his thought is of western origin. I hope that I did not give that impression.

Before he died he definitely had more work to do in integrating these two elements. He had not been given the opportunity to complete this work. It was certainly not a question of his merely taking western concepts in a mechanical fashion and then trying to affix Islamic labels to them. Any reading of his work will show that on the contrary he had in a real sense assimilated western philosophy, sociology, and thought -- by that I mean not simply that he knew what it was about, but that he understood its inner spirit. Precisely for this reason he was able to criticize it far more effectively than many other Muslim writers who have written in refutation of Marxism and content themselves with saying, "After all, Marx's father was a Jew. He was opposed to private property. He wanted to abolish the family. He did not believe in God." That is not a very convincing series of arguments in refutation of Marxism. Most other Muslim critics of Marxism have no real knowledge or control of the subject in the first place; whereas this was not so with Shari'ati. He fully assimilated these subjects and then moved to a refutation of them. He was not intimidated by them.

Many people in Islamic work who keep writing of the dangers of Marxism are terrified by it because they do not know what it is in the first place. Shari'ati knew what it was and was not afraid of it. This goes for the entirety of western thought. He was not a person who sought a mechanical joining of something from Islam and something from the West. He was a far more profound man than that.

I turn to your more general question -- should we take Qur'an first or modern social sciences? This is another of those false dichotomies. There is no programme laid down that first we read Qur'an and *sunnah* and then at a certain point we put them aside and take up textbooks on economics. Everything goes together.

There is a third element, which is more important: active involvement in some form of struggle. Otherwise it becomes a mere academic exercise of no value to anyone. At the risk of offending Indo-Pakistanis' sensibilities, why is there such a great air of unreality about many works of Maudoodi? It is because these are entirely intellectual works. They have not been written in the process of a revolutionary struggle. They are theoretical works that you feed to people, saying, "Come and get it. Follow this programme and everything will be OK." These are not ideas that are intermeshed with the living reality of a revolutionary struggle, which is one of the hallmarks of the work of Shari'ati. There we find the sense of vitality that comes from living commitment and not a mere intellectual exercise.

Dr Kalim Siddiqui: Did you say that Dr. Shari'ati translated from Franz Fanon?

HA: Yes.

Dr Kalim Siddiqui: I find it difficult that the Iranian intellectual scene needed the thoughts of Frantz Fanon and all of this school of thought in order to understand the Iranian situation, the whole of the Third World formulation in order to understand the imperialist system. Could it not have been done from the Muslim intellectual thought and sources alone, rather than going to Frantz Fanon, and so on?

HA: I did not mean to say that Frantz Fanon any more than any other writer was taken up by Shari'ati and incorporated into any system of thought. I was only saying that among the intellectual influences upon Shari'ati at a certain time in his life was Frantz Fanon.

We should not claim to have a monopoly of everything in the Muslim world. If we did have a monopoly of all that we needed for successful living in the contemporary world, the Muslim world would not be in the state it is in now. It is not enough to go on repeating in the form of a slogan "Quran, *sunnah*, Qur'an, sunnah ..." and forget everything else. Of course, we read Qur'an and *sunnah*, this is our basis. It is precisely because we do that, on the basis of Qur'an and *sunnah* we examine what else is available in the world, what other people are saying. In Shari'ati's case, what he derived from and maybe carried over into his own thought from the works of Fanon was the notion of alienation, the notion of cultural, psychological alienation and damage brought about by imperialism. I do not see what is the problem there. If no Muslim writer has written on the subject, why put Frantz Fanon in a corner because he is not a Muslim? If he has something interesting to say, why not take note of it and draw the necessary conclusions?

Dr Kalim Siddiqui: Coming to the literature of the Jama'at-e Islami, I do not really think that it is all theoretical. I think that it is deeply affected by the western literature on the emergence of the so-called democratic West, the consultative West, and therefore trying to say that the western civilization is really a latter-day branch of the original Islamic trunk. This is a major trend of thought among Muslims. Sir Sayyid Ahmad Khan and many others have propounded these thoughts. I feel that Maudoodi is a relevant figure in the progression of that apologist thought. Although he did not appear to be apologist, I think he was and is an apologist. His literature is relevant and very modern, rather than purely theoretical and old fashioned.

HA: When I use the word "theoretical" I did not mean to imply that it was totally devoid of any influence from the existing environment. I mean simply that it is not the result of an actual revolutionary struggle for the implementation of Islam. What you say is true. Maudoodi's works, whatever their merits -- and I do not mean to imply that they are totally without merit -- come in a certain tradition, which can be characterized as apologist. One of the most unconvincing books on birth control in Islam that I have ever read is Maudoodi's, since he fails to take the real issue that is the whole crux of the argument about birth control -- the necessity of lowering the population, and so on. Maybe it is a false argument, but if so the falsity needs exposing. He does not do this. Instead, he concentrates purely on the horrendous moral consequences if a means of birth control becomes freely available. In that book he is concerned more with criticizing what he perceives as the social reality of the western world than with addressing the problems of the Islamic world. Thus far he is correctly described as apologist.

Question: One of the latest slogans of Shari'ati was "Socialism, mysticism, and freedom." He changed it later to "Equality and mysticism." What is your comment?

HA: First, I shall have to see the evidence that this was so. It is the first time I have heard of it. His refutation of socialism is contained in the book 'Irfan, Barabari, Azadi, where there is a fairly comprehensive critique not only of Marxism but of western socialism — social democracy.[11] He does not use the words socialist and socialism in a positive sense at all. Even if he had used the word socialism instead of equality originally in the title of that book, it does not necessarily mean, as far as I can see from a reading of that book, that he espoused socialism, because in that book he is criticizing, among other things, the excessive emphasis given

---

[11] The English translation of this work -- "Mysticism, Equality, Freedom" - is to be found in Marxism and Other Western Fallacies, pp. 97-122.

in differing periods and in differing societies to each of these three elements. He says that each of them conceived correctly responds to a genuine human need, but they must be kept in balance, and so on, and this is what Islam does. He criticizes various schools of thought for failing to do precisely this, giving excessive emphasis to one of these three elements.

I have numerous reservations about many of the ideas of Dr. Shari'ati. But I find him more rewarding to read than many other contemporary Muslim writer, because he says, "I come to disquiet the quiet." The Muslim world is half asleep. You should be thankful that in Iran people have awoken. Nobody can deny that, right or wrong, one of the agents in this awakening was Dr. Shari'ati.

The year of the Revolution

ﻟﻤﺴﻜﺎﺑﺎﻳﻲﻏﻼﻳﻌﺎﻟﻤﺴ

W e come today, after considering certain of the important factors in the background of the Islamic Revolution, to consider the Revolution itself; that is, the series of events that began in January 1978, to use the Christian calendar, and terminated a little over a year later with the final removal of all traces of the Shah's regime in Iran and its substitution by a provisional Islamic revolutionary government. We have seen how there existed in Iran with growing intensity from the latter part of the nineteenth century onwards a tradition of opposition to the monarchy, the institution of the monarchy, and the foreign powers that stood behind it. This opposition was led, directed, and inspired by the most prominent of the Shi'i *ulama* in Iran. We have seen also, as the culmination and exemplary embodiment of that tradition, that there came to the fore the unique figure of Imam Khomeini, from 1962 onwards.

We have also seen how during the nearly fourteen years of his exile his influence was supplemented to some degree by the activity of Dr. Ali Shari'ati. Nonetheless, we need some further investigation to establish precisely why, at the beginning of 1978, a long tradition of agitation, discontent, and opposition turned into a revolutionary situation.

We can find throughout the years of the Shah's dictatorship numerous signs of all not being well in the so-called oasis of stability in the turbulent Middle East, this being the image the Shah and his propaganda agents sought constantly to create. But the signs of discontent multiplied throughout 1977. We saw, for example, in the summer of 1977 remarkable evidence that even on the material plane the Shah's regime had failed to create the so-called civilization that was offered. There were vast electricity failures in Tehran which in a way came to symbolize the inability of the regime to create the very simple infrastructure of a modern industrial economy that had been the great promise held out by the Shah. Together with this there was rising inflation, a soaring cost of living, not merely in the capital city, but in the major provincial cities and to some extent in the countryside. This economic discontent soon intensified the existing social and ideological discontent so that in the fall of 1977, shortly before one of the Shah's trips to the United States, there were a large number of demonstrations and open letters to the regime demanding, not yet abolition of the regime, but certain reforms.

We find, for example, that as one consequence of President Jimmy Carter's hypocritical election propaganda concerning human rights, people decided that this was a useful instrument to employ against the Iranian regime. It is sometimes said in America in the aftermath of the Islamic Revolution that Carter somehow undermined the Iranian regime by promising people human rights and that people, encouraged by President Carter, therefore took to the streets. This is an absurdity. A more accurate version of the situation is that it was seen as a useful tactic to demand human rights, not that the regime was deemed capable by its nature of giving human rights, but simply that given this apparent verbal change in American policy, the slogan of human rights was a useful one to be used for tactical purposes against the regime.

Similarly, the partial demands made by certain professional organizations of writers and lawyers calling for freedom of expression, the abolition of the restrictions of censorship, and the strict observance of the Iranian legal code all had the same purpose of tactically whittling away at the regime's position. None of this was new in the Iranian context and none of it was aimed at a totally comprehensive revolution, a sweeping away of the very foundations of the regime. It was a question of tactically harassing the regime in a fashion that might be thought to coincide with a new emphasis in American foreign policy.

In November 1977 the Shah of Iran visited the United States. The Shah had been visiting the United States continuously since his accession to power in 1941. In the American press at that time an interesting series of photographs appeared that showed the Shah in friendly conversation with every American president since Truman. A commentary supplied by an Iranian friend seemed apposite. He said that those pictures of the Shah shaking hands with every incoming president reminded him very much of the traditional political practice in Iran when the provincial governor at the accession of every new king would travel to the capital city, offer some appropriate present to the king, be confirmed by him in his position, and then be sent back to the province under his control to resume plundering and looting for his own profit and that of the central government. We can say that this is a very apposite comparison for the appearance of the Shah in Washington to swear allegiance to every new American president.

It turned out that this visit of the Shah to Washington was to be his final visit. It was one, moreover, that was overshadowed by unprecedented student demonstrations in America, so much so that the tear gas employed in putting down the demonstrations even drifted across the White House lawn and caused the Shah to shed a few tears. Despite the massiveness of the Iranian protest against the Shah on the threshold of the White House, Carter now undertook a total reversal of his policy and, far from criticizing the Shah or exercising pressure upon him to change his human rights policy, praised him in lavish terms, saying that there was complete identity of policy between the United States and Iran. This declaration of friendship and support to the Shah was repeated in even more exaggerated and fulsome terms when Carter visited Tehran. He said that he and the Shah saw eye to eye on the question of human rights -- an interesting confession on the part of Mr. Carter. These expressions of support were to be repeated throughout the year at strategic and crucial points by the Carter administration.

We find, for example, that immediately after the great massacre in Tehran on 8 September, 1978, when an estimated four thousand people were killed, Carter left his humanitarian efforts on behalf of so-called peace at Camp David to send a personal message of support to the Shah. It is noteworthy that Sadat and Begin and the other participants in these humanitarian efforts at Camp David also took time off to telephone their best wishes to the Shah in the aftermath of this massacre.

Given this timing of Carter's expression of support for the Shah, we can do no other than regard his visit to Tehran and his proclamation of support for the Shah at the beginning of 1978 as an implicit statement of support of the Shah and of all the acts of massacre and repression that he undertook in the year of the Revolution. It was not only a revolution, an uprising designed to shake and destroy the tyrannical rule of the monarch; it was at the same time in a real sense a war of independence waged against a power that had successfully turned Iran into a military base and that had incorporated the military, repressive apparatus of that other country into its own strategic system.

One of the errors that proved fatal for the Shah's regime and hastened its eventual downfall, an error that we may say from Muslim perspective was divinely determined, was that the Shah's regime in its arrogance caused a series of articles to be published insulting Imam Khomeini in the grossest and most obscene terms. They were published in the semi-official newspaper *Ittila'at* shortly after the visit of President Carter to Iran. In these articles it was claimed that Imam Khomeini was guilty of sexual deviance, that he was of Indian origin, which was meant in the terms of that Shah's regime and mentality to be an insult, and that he was an agent of British intelligence.

Such a series of accusations and fabrications is a common weapon in the armory of various tyrannical regimes in the Muslim world. In documents that have recently become available in various Iranian consulates and embassies around the world, we see that the Iran regime fabricated similar allegations to discredit the late Dr. Shari'ati. In another Muslim country, to engage in a brief diversion, we can see that recently the governments of Syria and Iraq have accused the Muslim Brethren of being traitors and the servants of Zionism and United States imperialism. This a familiar tactic. Its application in the case of Iran backfired totally against the regime.

Anger had already been aroused in November 1977 by the sudden death in Najaf, under unexplained circumstances, of Sayyid Mustafa Khomeini, eldest son of the Imam; this was widely regarded as one more crime of SAVAK. The open attack on the Imam that the newspaper articles constituted now caused this anger to reach a peak, especially in Qum, the same city where Imam Khomeini had studied and first risen to public prominence.

Immediately after the publication of the offending articles in the government-controlled press, demonstrations and protests broke out. The people of the city took to the streets denouncing not merely this latest affront of the Shah's regime all sense of humanity, Islam, and decency, but also the overall record of the regime. The answer of the regime was the usual one -- the massive use of force resulting in the loss of about two hundred lives. In this case, as in other subsequent cases, the exact number of casualties is difficult to determine.

After the events in Qum a cycle of recurring demonstrations, put down with heavy loss of life, began to be repeated. These gradually changed from being a series of isolated incidents in different parts of the country to a coordinated, unified movement, having not merely the negative aim of removing the Shah but the positive aim of establishing in the place of his regime an Islamic republic. Forty days after the martyrdom of the people of Qum, demonstrations and ceremonies of remembrance took place in the northwestern city of Tabriz, which is the capital of the large and populous province of Azerbaijan.

Tabriz has had a long history of prominence in Iranian revolutionary politics for various reasons, partly because of its proximity to Turkey and the Caucasus, which were in the early part of this century centers of revolutionary thought and activity. The demonstrations and commemorative ceremonies in Tabriz soon took on the complexion of a full-scale uprising, and for at least two days the entire city of Tabriz was out of control of the government forces.

The uprising was on a scale that the government had been unable to foretell. The local police and SAVAK proved unable to cope with the massive scale of the uprising and members of the local garrison also proved either unwilling or unable to intervene effectively. Reinforcements were then brought in from outside the city, but these were met by the people of the city themselves who pointed out that they were Muslims and it was the duty of the soldiers not to engage in the killing of their own brethren. This argument appears to have had an effect on a number of soldiers. Finally, the uprising in Tabriz was broken not so much by the use of the police or the army as by firing on the population from the air from military helicopters, gunships of the same type that the United States used repeatedly in Vietnam. Very heavy reprisals took place. It has been estimated that a minimum of five hundred people were killed in the course of the uprising in Tabriz.

In the aftermath of the Tabriz uprising, the Shah and his representatives claimed that the people of the city were in reality not participating in the uprising but that it had been a question of foreigners smuggled in in massive numbers to perpetrate this plot. It seems remarkable that thousands of Azerbaijani-speaking foreigners could be infiltrated into the city without detection. Another absurdity propagated by the regime and others associated with it was that the uprising in Tabriz had as its object the suppression of the Baha'i community. This was one line put out by the former American ambassador to Iran, William Sullivan, who happened to visit Berkeley shortly after the Tabriz uprising. The only problem, as one member of his audience pointed out, was that there is no Baha'i community in Tabriz of any significance for people to rise up in protest against. This same member of the audience further suggested that the traditional definition, by Samuel Johnson, of an ambassador or a diplomat should be revised. You may recall that Samuel Johnson defined a diplomat as a man who went abroad to lie for his country. In the case of Mr. Sullivan, it appeared that, on the contrary, the diplomat was the man who came home to lie on behalf of the government to which he had been accredited.

The uprising in Tabriz was followed soon after by the series of commemorative ceremonies in different cities of Iran. That also took on an aspect of minor insurrection. We can mention in particular the case of Yazd, where people emerging from a peaceful commemorative ceremony in one of the main mosques of the city were met with a hail of machine gun fire. A tape recording of these events was made and circulated widely throughout Iran. As anyone who has had occasion to hear this and similar tapes will know, it is a remarkable sequence of sounds which bears chilling witness to the brutality of the Shah's regime and its repressive methods.

On the tape one hears the termination of the *khutba* ending the commemorative ceremony, people emerging from the mosque into the streets, then the wail of police and army sirens, the opening of machine gun fire, and the wailing and screaming of the dying and the wounded. This tape, and the even more horrific tape made on the occasion of the government attack on the inside of a mosque several months later in Shiraz, should be required listening for all of those who have any lingering doubts concerning the nature of the Shah's regime.

We can say in passing that the cassette tape played a role of considerable importance in the Islamic Revolution. The Shah had a technological apparatus of repression of considerable sophistication. He had an army of four hundred thousand men, among the best equipped in the Middle East, second in military potential only to the other American - equipped killing machine, that of Israel. He had also a sophisticated repressive apparatus which had struck fear into the people for a quarter of a century. In contrast to this, the Iranian people had at their disposal very little in the way of armaments and organizational or technological capacity. The one thing that was used, and used to great effect, was the cassette tape.

Not only were recordings such as those I have mentioned circulated widely throughout Iran, but the declarations of Imam Khomeini were distributed throughout the country by a simple means, through the use of tape recording. I was a witness while in

Paris to the despatch of one such message to Iran. The simplicity of this apparatus of despatch and transmission of recorded messages was a source of astonishment to many western observers. All that happened was that the message would be recorded in Paris and read over the telephone to a number of individuals in Tehran who would have tape recorders held against the telephone. They would then telephone other individuals in provincial cities who were waiting with their tape recorders and in a brief time the message would be duplicated and circulated throughout the country.

Many people in the Middle East and South Asia will know how frequent it is for taxi drivers and truck drivers to go around with tape cassette players listening to the latest "pop" music. It was one symbol of the Islamic Revolution in Iran that the only tapes played in long-distance trucks, in buses, and in taxis were the tapes of Imam Khomeini. We can say that in one way the Revolution was a revolution of which the technological symbol was the cassette tape, just as earlier the Constitutional Revolution had been the revolution of the telegram. (Telegrams were sent back and forth between the Shi'i centers of Iraq and various cities in Iran).

To return to the chronology of events, after the uprising in Yazd and the heavy casualties inflicted there, we find for the first time in August major disturbances occurring in Tehran also. These obliged the Shah to cancel his projected European trip. On two occasions during the Revolution the Shah was obliged to cancel foreign trips. On both occasions the trips he had planned were to the Communist states of Eastern Europe. The incongruity of this situation was not perceived by most foreign journalists and observers, who persisted in the argument that the Shah was a bulwark of the West in the strategic struggle against Communism and that he was threatened by a communist-manipulated uprising at home. It was precisely Communist states he had been planning to visit when the uprisings broke out in Tehran. It was also a prominent Communist visitor, Hua Kuo Feng, the Chinese premier, who saw fit to come to Tehran and to fly by helicopter from the airport over the battle-torn streets of Tehran to confer with the Shah and offer him his condolences and his encouragement in the imperial struggle for progress and emancipation.

The month of August, not only because of the occurrence of large-scale disturbances in Tehran but also as a result of other events, saw a significant rise in the level of the struggle. It was in the month of August, to be precise on 19 August, that there took place the most infamous of the crimes of the Shah's regime, the burning of the Cinema Rex in the southwestern city of Abadan. You may recall that on that day the cinema was burnt to the ground, resulting in the deaths of some 420 people who were locked inside the cinema. This was billed in the western press as one of the fruits of the fanatical reactionary Islamic movement in the country, which was annoyed when people went to the cinema during the month of Ramadan. It is true that it was the month of Ramadan, a month of intensified religious feeling and struggle. It is also true that numerous cinemas had been burnt and destroyed throughout Iran by the Islamic movement.

However, there are two things to be noted here. The first is that in the case of the other cinemas that had been burnt, without exception advance warning had been given to the staff of the cinema to evacuate the premises in time, and a time had been chosen for the burning or the explosion when no showing was taking place and no audience was present in the cinema. Secondly, the film that was showing in Abadan was a film that obliquely and in a censored fashion referred to the activities of one of the guerrilla movements in Iran, the Sazman-i Mujahidin. This was therefore hardly a film likely to be found obnoxious by the Islamic movement as a whole. By contrast, in all the other cinemas that had been destroyed elsewhere, the film's shown were deemed offensive to the standards of Islamic morality.

Possibly the most telling piece of evidence -- and there is a large amount of evidence pointing to the responsibility of the regime for this arson -- is that not more than four days before the event the Shah had given a speech in which he said, "I promise you the great civilization; all that our enemies are capable of offering you is the great terror, *vahshat-i kabir*." It seems remarkably convenient that a few days later an event should occur that seemed to supply confirmation of this prediction -- that the great terror would be created.

The families of those burnt in the Cinema Rex were in any event not deceived by the government propaganda. Such was the extent of their protest and outcry that martial law had soon to be imposed on the city. In one grotesque instance of the humor that one finds recurring throughout the Revolution, the Cinema Rex in Abadan was bitterly nicknamed as the "Pahlavi kebab house." The people who had been burnt to death there were the direct victims of the Shah's regime.

The series of events that gained momentum throughout Ramadan, including the burning of the Cinema Rex, continued without letup into September so that the Shah began to make a number of outward concessions. He installed the government of Sharif Imami, who was widely praised in the western press, or at least described in the western press as a pious Muslim. You may know that this title of "pious Muslim" is given on a rather arbitrary basis by the western press. Someone who is from our point of view very obviously a Muslim and serving the interests of Islam is described as a reactionary and a fanatical Muslim. Someone who is willing to do the ways of the West is generally described as a pious Muslim. In this context, for example, Anwar Sadat is a pious Muslim, but Imam Khomeini is a fanatic or a reactionary Muslim.

In any event, Sharif Imami, because of certain family ties several generations back, was designated as a pious Muslim, and the Shah went through the gesture of removing certain Baha'is from his immediate entourage, abolishing the imperial calendar that he had introduced in substitution of the Islamic calendar, and promising a complete purge of the administration to remove all traces of corruption. The problem was that he was the greatest instrument of corruption and thus that promise was self-contradictory. As the Turkish proverb says, "When fish stinks, it stinks from the head first."

It was soon realized that the month of Muharram would be a crucial period in Iran. In anticipation of that month, which corresponded approximately to the month of December 1978, the Shah's regime made certain preparations. First of all, Sharif Imami was replaced by an outright military government under General Azhari. The immediate pretext for this was provided by successive days of riots and burning in Tehran when part of the British Embassy was burnt down and a number of other targets attacked. Shortly after, the Shah brought pressure upon the Iraqi government to expel Imam Khomeini from his longstanding place of exile in Najaf. We may regard this attempt to exile anew Imam Khomeini from the Islamic world as one of the great blunders of the Shah's regime. This turned out to be very much to the advantage of the Shah's opponents.

Imam Khomeini was harassed in Najaf by the Ba'athist regime -- not for the first time, by the way. There had been numerous instances over the years when he had been placed under pressure as a result of the Ba'athist regime's amenability to the Shah's desires. On this occasion, he was placed under virtual house arrest. His house was besieged and he was informed that he could continue to reside in Iraq only on two conditions: first, that he abandon all political activity, and secondly, that he move from Najaf to somewhere else of the Iraqi government's own choosing. These conditions were rejected by Imam Khomeini. The Iraqi government then proceeded to expel him from the country. The original plan, according to those in the entourage of Imam Khomeini, was that he should pass through Kuwait, there to embark for a further destination. Interestingly enough, the Kuwaiti government, which has a Ministry of Islamic Affairs, which publishes books on Islam, which hosts Islamic conferences and sends money for various mosques abroad, was so concerned about the promotion of "Islam" that it did not give permission to Imam Khomeini even for transit through its territory. As a result of this, Imam Khomeini remained for a few dangerous hours in the "no-man's-land" between Iraq and Kuwait, with neither government responsible for his safety.

After a time, the Iraqi government permitted him to re-enter the country on condition that he leave, and he left for Paris, which one can say was a remarkably fortunate choice. That is not to say that there is any particular virtue inherent in the French government, for no advance warning or notification was given to the French government. Imam Khomeini merely embarked on the plane and presented the French government with a fait accompli by arriving there with a valid Iranian passport and desiring to stay there for three months on a tourist visa. Of course, Imam Khomeini had a far more important task than tourism awaiting him in Paris. He took up residence in a house in the hamlet of Neauphle-le-Chateau outside Paris, which soon became a point of attraction for Iranians from Europe, North America, and Iran itself as well as a large number of representatives of the world's press.

It can be said without doubt that communication between Paris and Iran was infinitely more easy and swift and unimpeded than had been communication between Najaf and Iran. Also, Imam Khomeini was now able to bring the cause of the Iranian people more effectively before world public opinion.

The month of Muharram was described by Imam Khomeini in one of the proclamations that he issued from Neauphle-le-Chateau, as the month of triumph of blood over the sword. This one may regard in one way as a brief description of the Islamic Revolution in Iran. But it applies most particularly to Muharram in the sense that the willingness, the eagerness even, of the Iranian people for martyrdom during the month of Muharram, was manifested on a greater scale. A greater mass of people than ever before responded to the call of martyrdom which totally discredited and destroyed the basis of the Iranian regime.

From the first day of the month of Muharram a large number of people appeared in the streets of Tehran and other cities wearing their shrouds, preparing for martyrdom, and advancing unarmed on the rows of machine guns ready to shoot them down. The number of victims is difficult to establish precisely, but probably in the first few days of Muharram a larger total of people was killed than on any other occasion, with the single exception of Black Friday, 8 September 1978, massacre in Tehran.

One of the decisive turning points in the struggle after the burning of the Cinema Rex in Abadan had been the massacre that took place on 8 September in Tehran. This came shortly after the end of Ramadan, when a number of demonstrators were gathered in what was formerly called the Maydan-i Jaleh and is now called the Martyrs' Square in Tehran. A curfew had been proclaimed before there was the possibility of those gathered in the square learning of it and abiding by it, if they had chosen so to do. No chance was given to those gathered in the square to disperse. They were closed in on all four sides and soon the Shah's troops began firing from all four directions and from the air, from military gun ships. A tape recording of this horrendous occasion or part of its has also been made.

The slaughter lasted the better part of a day. A number of incriminating photographs are also available. On that occasion it was said that Israeli troops had participated in the work of massacre. In the nature of things it is not possible at present to have any decisive proof one way or the other. This much is certain: According to certain eyewitnesses of the event, one company of troops that stood in the forefront on that day had shown a reluctance to fire and it was swiftly removed and replaced by fresh troops dressed in Iranian uniforms. These troops spoke a language other than Persian and had an unkempt look, long beards and semihippy appearance. It might be said that the Shah's troops had shown little reluctance to slaughter people throughout the better part of the year and people might wonder why it should be necessary for the regime to have recourse to Israelis on this occasion. A possible answer is that in the week preceding this, from the end of Ramadan onwards a series of huge, indeed unprecedented demonstrations had taken place in Tehran, and the Shah may have regarded this as a crucial week in his struggle for survival. It may be that he thought it best to have at his disposal troops, mercenaries virtually, whose willingness to fire, even happiness in firing when their targets were Muslim, would not be called into question.

Whether that precise accusation be true, the fact that it was circulated and widely believed is an indication of the perception of the Iranian people of the deep involvement of Israel in the repressive apparatus and policies of the Shah.

To come from Ramadan to Muharram, from September to December 1978, the massive demonstrations that had taken place at the end of Ramadan were repeated on the two most crucial days -- ninth and tenth of the month -- which are in terms of the traditional Shi'i commemorative ceremonies of the martyrdom, the most important days. First, it was said by Azhari, the military premier, that a dawn-to-dusk curfew would be imposed and that no ceremonies would be allowed even in the mosque, let alone in the streets of the city. Then, when it was made clear that the people had no intention of observing this ban, gradually it was lifted and permission was given for a vast demonstration that took place along the major thoroughfares of Tehran, concluding at the so-called Shahyad monument -- the monument to twenty-five hundred years of Iranian monarchy. We may remark in passing on another instance of revolutionary humor in Iran, which was the renaming of the shahyad monument as the "*shayyad*" monument -- a monument not in memory or commemoration of the Shah but in commemoration of a "scoundrel." On this day the streets leading to the northern parts of Tehran where most of the royal palaces and the abodes of the wealthy are situated were sealed off and a vast number of people, estimated at between five million and six million, moved along the main arteries towards the square where a manifesto was read and approved by those present.

The manifesto called for the abolition of the monarchy, for the institution of an Islamic republic and the observance of certain points relating to internal and external policy. There was a total of sixteen points. President Carter, in one of the foolish remarks for which he is becoming increasingly celebrated, said that the fact that the day had passed off without bloodshed was somehow a triumph for the Shah's regime and an indication that, after all, things would not be too bad and he could weather the storm, as he had weathered previous storms. The fact that there had been no bloodshed was uniquely the result of the nonintervention of the army on that day. It was a moral triumph for the Islamic movement and a stunning defeat for the Shah.

It became increasingly recognized by the Shah, and more importantly by his foreign advisers, that his was a lost cause and that the best that could be hoped for was the installation of what was called in American terminology a compromise solution -- that is to say, neither the Shah nor the Islamic regime but something in between led by "moderate, reasonable people"; in other words, people who would be content to see a prolongation of American strategic domination in Iran.

After some hedging and looking around for a suitable candidate, in late December the candidate was decided upon, Shapur Bakhtiar, the leader of the National Front, who was immediately promoted in western propaganda as being a longstanding foe of the Shah, a leading member of the opposition, a champion of human rights, and all other kinds of high-sounding titles.

It should be pointed out that the National Front, particularly as it had come to exist in recent years in Iran, was not a major organ of opposition to the Shah. It had a certain weight and represented a certain number of interests, but it was not in any way an important organization of political opposition such as it had been in the days of Dr. Musaddiq. Even within the attenuated National Front Shapur Bakhtiar had a very dubious standing. There were a number of incidents in which he was involved that had earned him the suspicion of his associates, so much so that when he accepted the offer of the Shah at the prompting of the United States to become the new prime minister, with the Shah going on vacation, members of the National Front and still less the Iranian people at large were not surprised.

Shapur Bakhtiar arranged for the departure of the Shah, which took place in January 1979, and then began the hopeless task of attempting to shore up the foundations of his own power. Whatever the failings of Shapur Bakhtiar, and they are numerous, he was obviously a man not totally without intelligence. One of the intriguing questions that, to my mind, has not yet been fully answered is why Bakhtiar chose to take on this hopeless task of saving the American cause in Iran after the departure of the Shah in mid-January. The only interim answer that can be given to that question is that he was a man, above all else, totally contemptuous of religion and, therefore, like many other secularists, he assumed that religion had no effective power. Because he did not believe in it, he thought ipso facto nobody else sincerely believed in it either and therefore it should be discounted as an effective force.

We can say that this kind of assumption is shared in general by many members of the Iranian bourgeoisie. They thought, "Let the revolution go through, let the rebellion be led for the time being by the *ulama*. After all, these people are not people of the world and they are politically naive; and we, the secular bourgeoisie, the western-educated, the liberal intelligentsia, will assume our natural right of leadership in due time."

Something of the same mentality in a rather extreme form was present in Bakhtiar, I think. He was incautious enough to describe Imam Khomeini as "an insane old man." It was precisely this "insane old man" who totally outmanoeuvred and destroyed the regime of Bakhtiar within less than a month of its installation. At the beginning of February 1979, after a series of political manoeuvres on the part of Bakhtiar and the Iranian army, including the closure of Tehran airport for a number of days, Imam Khomeini returned to a triumphal welcome by the people of Iran. It has been estimated that on this occasion about one third of the total population of Iran was in Tehran to receive him. A number of cities in the country were almost completely emptied as their inhabitants converged on Tehran to give a triumphal welcome to Imam Khomeini.

He returned and, in accordance with his proclaimed intention, proceeded immediately to the cemetery in Tehran where the martyrs of the Revolution were buried and gave one of his typically courageous and uncompromising speeches, denouncing the United States for its role during the Revolution, saying that the Iranian people had desired freedom and that they had been given in exchange by imperialism and its agents a graveyard full of martyrs as the answer to their demand. He pointed out also that the struggle was not yet over, and he summoned the Iranian people to continue in their struggle.

Four days after his return Imam Khomeini named his own government -- the provisional government headed by Mehdi Bazargan. Progressively, ministers were named to complete the cabinet. This was a process that continued after the final triumph of the Revolution. In the two weeks between the return of Imam Khomeini and the final overthrow of the regime the crucial question appeared to many people to be the possibility of an American-inspired and directed military coup d'etat. The great fear of numerous people was precisely this. After all, the United States had been heavily involved in Iran to a degree unparalleled virtually in any other country. Doubtless it must have had some contingency planning for a day such as that now dawning in Iran. Would the United States easily abandon the strategic, economic, and military advantages that it had enjoyed in Iran for a quarter of a century?

Anxiety was increased by the arrival in Tehran of the commander of the American land forces in Europe, General Robert Huyser. The ostensible purpose of his visit to Tehran was to discuss the problems of arms supply in the aftermath of the disturbance and uprising in Iran, and also to dissuade the Iranian military from attempting a coup d'etat. It seems that the time, just over a month, that he spent in Tehran was rather a generous period of time for dealing with these limited objectives.

Since the triumph of the Revolution, documentary evidence has been uncovered to the effect that the purpose of Huyser's visit to Tehran was, on the contrary, to undertake a contingency study of the possibility of a military coup d'etat. His departure from the country should be taken as a sign that the study had yielded negative results, that at least in the short term the possibility of a military coup d'etat successfully imposing itself was extremely limited.[1] The Iran of 1979 was no longer the Iran of 1953. After all, the Iranian army had become subjected to increasing desertions by its

[1] Confirmation is now available in Huyser's own memoirs, *Mission to Tehran* (London, 1986).

recruits; considerable psychological pressure had been exerted by the religious leadership headed by Imam Khomeini, who repeatedly called for the army to return to the people to which it essentially belonged. At the same time, it was known that the people were arming in such a fashion that a military coup d'etat would not have been unopposed.

It was, fittingly enough, the most recalcitrant elements in the army that brought about the final downfall of the last vestiges of the Shah's regime. On 10 February 1979, in one of the air force barracks in Tehran, air force cadets were engaged in watching an Iranian television replay of the newsreel film showing the return to Tehran of the Imam Khomeini. As a result of watching this film, they broke out into demonstrations demanding the installation of an Islamic government under Imam Khomeini. Their officers insisted that they return to barracks, instead of which they raided the armory and resisted by armed force. The commanders of the garrison called in the Imperial Guard, the so-called eternal or immortal guard, the so-called crack troops of the Shah, to aid in the task of repression. A number of tanks arrived very quickly at the air force garrison.

The beginning of this battle was the sign for an armed uprising throughout Tehran, which resulted in the overrunning, one after another, of all the major installations of power, the prime minister's office, radio and television, the parliament building, the headquarters of SAVAK and its various interrogation and torture centers throughout the city; so that after two or three days, which saw a minimum of seven hundred to eight hundred further casualties, the regime of the Shah was finally swept away in the last bloodbath.

This has been an approximate retelling of the important events of the Revolution. Of course, many details have been left out, but I think that I have given you a sketch of the most important events. It is time now, by the way of ending this lecture and the series of lectures generally, to try to draw a few conclusions which are, I think, of particular relevance to Muslims and which will, I hope, illustrate the contention I made at the beginning of my first lecture, namely, that the events in Iran are the most important and significant events for the entire Muslim world in recent history. They are not in any way an isolated series of events determined by the circumstances of Iran.

First of all, I pointed out that the movement of the Iranian Muslim people was opposed unanimously by all the major superpowers and their agents in the region. One can think of this as a simple and automatic test of the authenticity of any Islamic movement. If any Islamic movement finds itself allying, even circumstantially and unintentionally, with a major power, there is a certain problem. It means that there is some willingness to compromise, to settle, to collaborate with a non-Islamic power, or there is the perception that it is willing to do so.

The Islamic Revolution in Iran was opposed by the United States, the Soviet Union, China, Great Britain, West Germany, France -- by all these major centers of power and corruption in the world. Within the Middle Eastern region, it was opposed with varying degrees of active engagement by the so-called reactionary regimes and so-called progressive regimes alike. It was opposed by King Hasan of Morocco, who described the Imam Khomeini as a naive old man and who sent his special envoy to speak to some of the Iranian *ulama* to persuade them that they should not fall into the trap of communism. It was opposed by President Sadat of Egypt, who had displayed to the world now his policy of capitulation in his search for a personality and identity, something that he clearly lacks and has little chance of finding.[2]

The movement was opposed by the Saudi regime which, for all its sponsorship of Muslim conferences and its claim to be a fit custodian of the Haramayn, is clearly at the service of the United States and opposed to all vital manifestations of Islam in the Islamic world. On the side of the so-called progressive regimes, it was opposed by the Iraqi government, the Ba'athists, who are meant to be the ultra hard-line rejectionists in terms of the current

---

[2] An allusion to the title of Sadat's autobiography, *Bahth 'an al-Dhat: Qissat Hayati* (Cairo, 1978).

political jargon. It was opposed by Libya; let there be no doubt about that. Qadhdhafi was opposed to the Shah, but he was not in any way favorable to the Islamic movement in Iran until it became clear that it was about to triumph. The only support given by Qadhdhafi was to a Marxist guerrilla group called Fidayan-i Khalq and to the separatist movement in Kurdistan. It is interesting that recently Qadhdfhafi has also come out in favor of Kurdish nationalism, the secession of Kurdish areas of Iraq and Iran to form a separate and independent state.

In short, there was this alliance of the great powers and their regional satellites arrayed against the Islamic Revolution. We may say that this is at once a proof of the authenticity of the Revolution and a warning that when any genuine Islamic movement comes into being it will be faced with similar opposition. Yet it was precisely in the face of such opposition that the Islamic movement in Iran triumphed. To find an explanation for this in terms purely of the familiar means of political and historical analysis is impossible. When Imam Khomeini was asked, about the causes for the success of the Revolution, he said simply that it was the will of God. The will of God manifests itself through causes that are capable of being analyzed, but we as Muslims believing in Islam as a total view of reality, a set of methods for the understanding of reality, should say that the triumph of the Islamic Revolution was indeed the fulfillment of God's promise, which remains eternally valid to those who struggle in His path, irrespective of secondary and contingent causes.

At one point, Imam Khomeini was asked while in Paris asked him, "Do you not think there is a danger of this continual bloodshed and sacrifice on the part of our people inducing despair and weariness in them so that the point of our movement will become lost? Might it not be better to pause, to have some temporary arrangement seeking a reform of the existing regime?" Imam Khomeini replied simply that it is our task to do that which Allah tells us to do and it is then up to Allah whether He supplies the results in our lifetime or in a future lifetime. It was as a result of this trust in Allah, of this solitude with Allah, this deprivation of any form of worldly support and this reliance on the support of Allah -- a reliance that was clearly testified through the embrace of martyrdom by not less than fifty thousand people in the year of struggle -- that ultimately the Revolution in Iran was able to succeed.

The second general conclusion we as Muslims should draw from the Revolution is the fact that the crucial factor in the success of the movement is not sophistication of organization. It is not the working out of any precise strategic plan that is crucial, although at various points in the struggle questions of strategy of course assume importance. It has often been said that in Iran we have a hierarchy of Shi'i *ulama* that is lacking elsewhere in the Muslim world and therefore this triumph is not easily to be duplicated elsewhere.

What is meant by this so-called hierarchy of Shi'i *ulama*? There is, of course, the simple mechanism of *taqlid*, which I attempted to describe for you in my first lecture, whereby the individual believer regards himself as duty-bound to follow the guidance of a religious leader. This guidance is given on the basis of a moral and spiritual authority that is gained exclusively on the basis of popular assent. There is no electoral process for the choice of the *marja* or the *mujtahid*. It is simply that an individual, or series of individuals, emerge, who in themselves come to command the obedience of the believers. Naturally, the appeal and authority of Imam Khomeini by far transcended the mechanics of *taqlid*.

It is not inconceivable that a comparable development should take place in the Sunni Muslim world.[3] If there emerges a leader or a movement which clearly presents itself as a totally uncompromising and radical alternative to the existing system or systems, if it shows itself not concerned merely in a theoretical sense but in a practical sense with the actual, tangible problems of the people, there is no reason why it should not be able to elicit the same response as that which was elicited by Imam Khomeini from the Iranian people.

---

[3] It must be conceded that such a development has still not occurred, and structural factors would seem to militate against it for the foreseeable future.

Why is it that in Iran today we see the only genuine experiment in the foundation of an Islamic state in which we can have some confidence and hope? It is not because the Iranians as compared with other Muslim peoples are gifted with a superior degree of piety. It is not because they have discovered some particular secret that is inaccessible to the rest of the Muslim world. Certainly, it is not so. Let us not forget that Islam remains the prime motive force, at least in potentiality if not in actuality, of all the Muslim peoples without exception, whether they be Arabs, Turks, the peoples of the Indo-Pakistan sub-continent, Southeast Asia, Africa, or any other group of Muslims. Ultimately, it is not possible to eradicate Islam from the hearts of the Muslims. It is possible only to annihilate the Muslims themselves. Given that, what is necessary is to activate this resource of faith, belief, readiness to struggle, and sacrifice. This is something that is present within the hearts of all the Muslim peoples and even within the hearts of many individuals who are apparently secularized.

One of the things that happened in the course of the Islamic Revolution in Iran was the rediscovery of Islam by those who were partially secularized. I have described one aspect of this process in my lecture on Dr. Shari'ati, but it was not merely an intellectual process. It was also a question of individuals returning to their own selves, their cultural and historical identities. It is possible to operate a similar process in other Muslim countries, with the overwhelming majority of people, including many of those who apparently are lost to Islam. It is possible by the presentation of a clear, radical, complete and serious alternative that has no connection with the existing system, that does not wish to participate in it, does not enter it on the pretext of reforming it, but stands totally apart from it.

This leads me to one more conclusion concerning the Islamic Revolution -- that an Islamic movement will not only be automatically opposed by all the major superpowers and their local agents, but also, to be authentic and to have any chance of success, such a movement must be uncompromising in its ultimate goals. There comes a time when to be uncompromising is the only realistic course. It is not realistic to be moderate and compromise for an Islamic movement. For an Islamic movement to enter into so-called realistic compromises means, in effect, the sacrificing of its own nature and ultimate goals. There are too many examples of this for it to be overlooked. We may mention the example of Turkey, where a so-called Islamic party, which contains many people of great sincerity, energy, and devotion, has decided to enter the parliamentary game for the sake of promoting the Islamic interests. We see that precisely through entering the parliamentary game it begins playing all the familiar parliamentary tricks, beginning with the swearing of an oath of allegiance to the secular republic. It is not possible for this party in this situation, or similar parties in a similar situation elsewhere in the Islamic world, to present itself as opposed to the system in which it participates, and, therefore, in the survival of which it has a partial interest.

There is one other conclusion. It is that the Islamic movement, if it be correctly identified with the popular interests and not kept on the plane exclusively of pure ideology, if it be an uncompromising one that refuses any form of participation in the existing system, if it does this, it will be totally able to outdistance any forms of secular competition. One of the great differences between 1953 and 1979 in Iran is that in 1953 there was a Musaddiq and in 1979 there was a Khomeini. There was an Islamic involvement in the events leading up to the nationalization of the Iranian oil industry in 1953. But the secular figure, Musaddiq, overshadowed religious figures on the scene, such as Imam Kashani. Precisely because of this, the nationalist movement of Dr. Musaddiq could never be a mass movement with profound roots.

In 1978-79, we see on the contrary the so-called secular opposition, the National Front, with people like Sanjabi and the rest of them being totally overshadowed by the religious leadership. To have any form of political influence, the secular opposition was obliged to abandon its positions and to conform unconditionally to the demands advanced by Imam Khomeini. Similarly, in all other Muslim countries other forms of ideology and political organization, whatever inroads they may apparently have made, have largely failed to penetrate the depths of the hearts and minds of the Muslim people. Even though they may appear to be competitors for the future of the Muslim *ummah,* if correctly confronted, there is nothing to be feared from them. This is something that goes also for the purveyors of the secular nationalism and ethnic based nationalism in the Arab world, in Turkey, and elsewhere. It also goes for the Marxists. It is only the Islamic movement, the potential and not necessarily the actual Islamic movement, in various Muslim countries that has the ability to call upon the deepest resources of the people and bring about a genuine revival and renewal.

Any attempt to formulate a path to the future for the Muslim peoples other than with Islam, is ultimately a waste of time and energy and a waste of the most precious of our human and material resources. To prevent that waste the Islamic movements elsewhere must learn the fundamental lessons of the Islamic Revolution in Iran. Otherwise they will contribute to the state of ideological and spiritual anarchy that persists in the Muslim world. Unfortunately, the signs that the leaders, or at least the self-appointed leaders, of Islam in other countries are ready to learn from the Islamic Revolution in Iran are not very bright.

Let us take two examples. I saw recently an issue of an Islamic magazine called *Hilal* published in Turkey by a certain Salih Ozcan, who is significantly the representative of Turkey on the Rabitat al-Alam al-Islami. This magazine was published in March, one month after the triumph of the Islamic Revolution in Iran, and yet it did not include a single word on the subject of Iran. Similarly, in Pakistan the magazine *Criterion,* which is affiliated to the Jama'at, also has been revived recently. Its first issue appeared after a long period of interruption, and it did not contain a word about the tumultuous events in Iran.

There is a great responsibility, not only upon the Muslim leaders and the Muslims at large to learn the lessons of the Islamic Revolution, but also upon the leaders of the Revolution to communicate their experience to the Islamic world as a whole. There are signs that this responsibility is perceived in Iran and that steps are being undertaken to fulfill it. It is too soon to predict with any confidence the future course of events in Iran. There are grave problems now being confronted in that country, which are to be anticipated and which are not as grave or as fatal as the western press makes out. They are, nonetheless, real problems demanding real solutions. It is also far too soon to say what will be the ultimate impact of the Revolution on other Muslim countries. Whatever be the future turn of events in Iran and other Muslim countries, there is no doubt that what has already occurred in Iran is at the same time the most unexpected and the most joyful triumph of the Islamic *ummah* in the present century.

Discussion

Question: One is very concerned about the debate in Iran. What I do not understand is the attitude of the religious leaders of the so-called minorities, the Arabs and the Kurds, and so on. These people are demanding separation now. Under the Shah they kept quiet. Now that the Islamic Revolution has taken place and we are all saying "we are Muslims," they are going out against the Revolution. We hear, at least in the British press, that the religious leaders of these minorities are demanding emancipation. Could you comment on that?

HA: In the case of Kurdistan, the allegedly religious leader who is the most celebrated as demanding the segregation or autonomy of Kurdistan is a certain 'Izz ad-Din Husayni. He has been described as the Marx of Kurdistan since he is evidently on good terms with the leftists in the area. Additionally, he is said to have been on good terms with SAVAK before the Revolution. One of the common transformations following the Revolution is that former supporters of the monarchy have become Marxists. This is one of the forms in which counterrevolution is now seeking to mask itself in Iran. The case of Husayni, who is one of the so-called religious leaders of the Kurds in Iran, may be a case in point.

As to the other leaders of the Kurds in Iran, I do not think there are any persons even claiming religious prominence among them. The Kurds in Iran, as elsewhere, are fragmented. There is no single united Kurdish leadership with authority to speak for the Kurds of a single region, let alone for all the Kurds or all the Kurdish inhabited areas. As to Khuzistan, there is this Khaqani who is described as the religious leader of the Arab-speaking minority. I do not know anything about the history of this man, whether he was in any way active under the Shah's regime, nor do I know what effective control he exercises over people in Khuzistan demanding autonomy.

The problem that has arisen in Kurdistan and Khuzistan and even in the Baluchi-inhabited areas of the southeast is that the people have legitimate grievances. They have grievances inherited from the time of the Shah. They have the same grievances as the Persian-speaking majority in Iran; that is, they were neglected and oppressed for a number of years. In addition, they have certain grievances particular to themselves. For years it was forbidden in Iran to use languages other than Persian for any purpose apart from oral communication, whether the language be Azerbaijani, Turkish, Kurdish, Arabic, Baluchi, or whatever. In addition, certain minority-inhabited areas were worse off economically than others. A particularly glaring example was in Khuzistan, which was the source of the major wealth of the country through the oil industry. One finds that the oil workers in Abadan, most of whom are Arab ethnically speaking, lived in the most miserable conditions. After the revolution, these people naturally are impatient to see that their grievances are remedied.

This type of impatience one finds not only among the ethnic minorities but in many other sectors. One of the constant appeals of both Imam Khomeini and Bazargan is for "revolutionary patience" -- patience under the existing circumstances, with people not pressing a class or sectional grievance at a time when there are important general questions to be dealt with.

Taking advantage of this situation in the minority-inhabited areas are enemies of the Revolution, both domestic and foreign. They will move in to build up matters to a point of no return. So far matters have been more or less contained in Khuzistan and Kurdistan. In future I do not know how soluble these problems will prove to be. I do not think it is true to say that the religious leaders, whether in Kurdistan or Khuzistan, as a whole are behind the various agitations.

Question: Can you tell us something of the organizational aspect of the movement with regard to its membership, selection of members, training and the strategy, especially with regard to the Islamic Revolutionary Council?

HA: You are touching here on different matters. You speak about the movement, on the one hand, and the Revolutionary Council on the other. As for what we call in broad terms the movement, people should not be under the illusion that this is question of a formally organized movement with membership criteria, and so forth. Perhaps this is another lesson of the Revolution -- that it was a broad-based Islamic movement and not some kind of affair in which people sit down, as an examining body, and decide who is worthy to be admitted. What is necessary is to recruit in an informal fashion the massive support of the overwhelming majority of the people. This is what happened in Iran. It is not that a secret party or organization was set up which brought more and more people into the fold. There were some organizations, the guerrilla organizations, which engaged in urban warfare against the Shah's regime for a number of years. This is not what made the revolution. The revolution was genuinely a people's movement. One can say that the Islamic Revolution in Iran was an example of mass political participation, unique in modern times. It makes the parliamentary elections of the western countries appear as a mere game by contrast. In the United States a minority of the electorate turned out at the last election, and yet that is celebrated as an expression of the popular will. In Iran, in the face of massive pressure, the danger of death, dismemberment, and torture, a whole nation took to the streets to enforce its demands. This massive, almost elemental event, has more in common with some natural cataclysm than with a common political happening. This cannot be the result of any broad strategic plan.

As I attempted to indicate, the organizational structure of the Revolution is extremely simple. It was a question of the directives given by Imam Khomeini being distributed throughout Iran and then evoking an immediate response of obedience from the mass of the people. This is what it comes down to. Then we have the logistics involved, the planning of mass demonstrations. There were mass demonstrations where people were organized and arrangements were made for feeding them, and so on.

The Shah, in one interesting comment after the demonstrations, said, "This superb organization with which these demonstrations have been planned shows that there is foreign and communist involvement." He had such a low opinion of his own people that he thought they could not organize a demonstration without foreign involvement. He was reflecting his own mentality. He could not take a single step without instructions from Washington, London, or Moscow.

There is no organizational strategic mystery. The mosque was the fundamental unit of the organization. Perhaps this is a conclusion that I should have worked into my body of conclusions. One of the important elements in the success of the Revolution was the revival of the mosque, of the full dimensions and functions of the mosque, not simply as a retreat from society where people go to be away from the world and pray and make their ablutions and listen to the recitation of the Qur'an; on the contrary, it became a center of struggle, of organization and command. In short, it was all that it was in the time of the Prophet, upon whom be peace.

Comment: This is an important point because the difference between the Shi'i areas and what we have in the Sunni countries is marked. In the latter, the mosque is led by the man who is employed by the government and he is allowed only to speak about morals and ethical matters. Unfortunately, we cannot expect any movements emanating from the Arab countries to come from the mosques. It will also have to be from outside the main traditional centers of learning such as the religious universities. These have been completely depoliticized. They deal only with certain things and issue declarations supporting the king or the leader.

HA: It occurs to me that perhaps there is the necessity for the creation in the Islamic world of the phenomenon that the Muslims have brought about in the Soviet Union, namely, the underground or unauthorized mosques. In an interesting piece of research published by some French scholars, it was established that besides the approximately three hundred official mosques existing in the Soviet Union, there are many thousands of unofficial underground or unauthorized mosques that have been the true means for the survival of Islam in the Soviet Union. Whereas in the officially recognized mosques you will hear the *khutba* about the compatibility of socialism and Islam and the desirability of improving the output of the collective farm, and so on, in the underground mosques you will hear something quite different. Perhaps we should forget our obsession with nice domes and minarets and create underground mosques that are not mosques architecturally, but in spirit are indeed true mosques.

Comment: This phenomenon of government-controlled mosques is more typical of Arab countries. It is not true of countries of the Indo-Pakistan sub-continent and Southeast Asia.

Dr Kalim Siddiqui: It is true that this does not apply in all Sunni countries. For historical reasons, on the subcontinent where Muslims were rulers for eight hundred years, comparatively very few mosques were built. But during the last hundred and fifty years of colonial rule, Muslims built more mosques because there was little else for them to do. These mosques are not run by the government of Pakistan, Bangladesh, or India. Each little mosque is an autonomous unit, which supports an imam, a muezzin, and a number of others. Each has a catchment area for which it provides education, prayers, and ritual services. They have become very active at some point in time, such as in 1857 in India and during the Pakistan movement in the 1940s.

Comment: The most important factor we have to take into consideration is that people have had to be ready to sacrifice themselves for Islam and give their lives for it. This is a thing we have to learn -- that youth has to give all of its energies to Islam and if this does not happen all these other things begin to take place. We can take over the mosques, but we have to go there and work in them. This is the problem. People do not go to the mosque. How can they effect changes in the mosque?

HA: It is certainly true that there is nothing to be achieved without sacrifice.

Dr. Kalim Siddiqui: Would you not like to go on and comment on the lifestyle that is brought about by western education? There are people who believe in God, who believe in Islam, but above all who believe in their career and their personal advancement, the bank balance, the mortgage, their wife and family, and the bungalow. They come in and pray five times a day, but if you ask them for $5 a month they would rather give you their life. It would be easier to sacrifice their life. This is where the Islamic Cultural Center in London comes in. The center is a cathedral, a showpiece, an apologia for the Muslim governments of the world. It is not there to serve Islam. The trustees are the ambassadors of these Muslim countries. Instead of trying to stage a coup and reform that place, or any other place like it, we have to establish our own alternative institutions and bypass those people. Let us show them to be as irrelevant as they are.

Question: We have heard in the western press before the Revolution about the strikes and the different pressures brought upon the Shah's regime. Would you comment on that?

HA: I should certainly have mentioned the strikes, particularly the strikes of the oil workers which caused the income of the Shah to shrink and which were supplemented by the strikes of workers, in other sectors of industry and within the civil service so that the country was virtually on a permanent general strike. This was an important supplementary lever of pressure. One thing said in the western press was that the communists or leftist elements were strongly entrenched in the Iranian oil industry in particular.

I can recall Mr. Schlesinger, the then-American Secretary of Energy, predicting that Khomeini would be unable to get the oil workers to go back to work. In part, such distortions arise from pure and simple malice. They also arise from the fact that the very phrase "workers' committee" tends to arouse in the western mind the image of some Marxist agitator. The workers' councils that came into being in Iran, not only in the oil industry but in other branches of industry and in government offices, were largely Islamic in their orientation and were commonly led by religious figures. After the triumph of the Revolution in Iran, the oil industry commenced functioning again at precisely the time that Imam Khomeini appealed to the people to go back to work. It is not accurate to speak of an important communist presence. The whole subject of communism poses a separate question of some interest that might be gone into at some time.

One of the important things that has happened since the Revolution in Iran is that the communists -- and here I use the term in a general fashion to mean not only the official, Moscow-oriented party but the Marxist left in general -- have come to realize the very narrow nature of their support. It is precisely for this reason that they are continuously agitating in industry to try to get the workers out on strike again. They are meeting with very little success. They are attempting to fasten on to various secondary issues and make them their own. One example was the so-called women's demonstration that took place in Tehran. Another was the leftist movements in the minority-inhabited areas. The leftists have been involved in these "issues," attempting to compensate for their lack of appeal to those whose interests they supposedly espoused, namely, the working class and the peasants.

Question: In relating the chronology of the events of the Islamic Revolution, you spoke of the comments of President Carter and in your conclusion you cited the opposition of the major powers as evidence of the authenticity of the Islamic movement. I wonder whether you could spend a minute or two on the Soviet role? I believe it must have been one of opposition throughout, but somewhere it must have changed, superficially, to one of support for Khomeini.

My second question concerns the satellites of the great powers and their attitudes to the evolution. Can you spend some time on Pakistan? We know that President Zia went across to Iran in late 1978 and that Pakistan was the first state to recognize the new regime. Is there some duplicity here?

HA: As to the Soviet Union, what you say is true. The Soviet Union, as late as November 1978, gave its support to the Shah's regime. If you read the articles and commentaries that appeared in *Pravda*, you will see that in their tone and content they were almost identical with those in the *New York Times*, saying that the Shah was a likeable and impressive man and such things. It was in December that the Soviet Union, a little ahead of the United States, began to see the hopelessness of the Shah's position and gradually began to describe the events in Iran in a more positive light, although still underestimating the Islamic movement and suggesting that the role of Imam Khomeini would be merely a transitional one, heralding the genuine revolution, that is, a communist revolution. It gave orders to the Tudeh Party, which has been loyal to Moscow since its inception, to change its policies. Accordingly, one had the incongruous spectacle of members of the party being instructed to give an affirmative vote in the referendum to an Islamic republic. More recently, in the demonstrations against the enemies of the Revolution, domestic and foreign, the Tudeh Party was in there, carrying banners proclaiming support for the Islamic Revolution. Even more than the rest of the left, the Tudeh Party is a spent force in Iran. It is not taken seriously.

As for Pakistan, I think you have answered your own question. It was a rhetorical question, not requiring any answer from me. As you say, General Zia went to Iran and went through the customary bow in front of the Shah and then like many other people, attempted to change course rather abruptly after the triumph of the Revolution. Instead of being harsh on the Pakistan government, we should point out that this kind of sudden volte-face was not in the least confined to Pakistan. We find so-called Islamic organizations doing the same things.

In the United States, the Muslim Students' Association (MSA), which consistently sought to undermine any form of propagandistic activity by the Iranian students in America and those associated with them, suddenly transformed its attitude into a defense of the Islamic Republic after the downfall of the Shah. It is correct to say that the Jama'at-e Islami in Pakistan was extremely late in sending even a message of verbal support to Imam Khomeini. Not until December of last year did this happen. This duplicity, unfortunately, is not confined to Zia-ul Haq of Pakistan. It is the attitude of a certain mentality in the Muslim world that we find in a broad spectrum of persons, governments and movements.

Comment: I suggested to the Islamic Cultural Center, here in London, that they should hold a meeting to celebrate the Islamic Revolution. They said, "No! They are paid by governments. They do not celebrate the Islamic Revolution!"

HA: More serious is the fact that the Saudis arrested a number of people who were distributing one of the proclamations of Imam Khomeini, as part of their general mismanagement of the Haramayn. And that was not the first occasion.

Question: Do you not think that there is a need to point out that the acceptance of the political party system by various Islamic movements as Islamic is in fact an importation from the West? It is divisive and creates similar problems as we have seen in the west.

HA: This is true because the assumption of the parliamentary system presents a variety of permanently interchangeable alternatives. One of the slogans of the Islamic Revolution was "Our leader is Khomeini and our party is the party of Allah." This fragmentation of political life into competing parties, although it may be a reality at present, is not something that should be endowed with permanency.

Dr. Kalim Siddiqui: I now rise to close this meeting and with it to end the course. Those of us who have sat through these four lectures wish to thank Professor Hamid Algar for the great learning and erudition he has displayed, together with a total command of his subject. We are grateful for the great patience and scholarship that he has shown in presenting his material.

Today, Professor Algar, you have brought out ten conclusions from the Islamic Revolution in Iran. Each one was precisely formulated and concisely presented.

I thank Allah for everything He has made possible for us. We are a small, independent institute and you are a professor, and we have come together in this venture and successfully concluded it. I thank you once again, I thank Allah, and I thank our students for their participation.

Extracts from the Writings and Pronouncements of Imam Khomeini

CONCERNING THE DIFFERENCE BETWEEN KNOWLEDGE AND BELIEF

This extract is taken from Sharh-i Chihil Hadis *(Tehran, 1371 Sh.1982, pp. 37-38) a voluminous work explaining in detail forty hadith of the Prophet and the Imams (upon whom be peace), mostly on ethical and mystical topics, written by Imam Khomeini in 1938. The subject matter reflects the concerns that were central at the time to his teaching and writing activities.*

Know that belief is different from the knowledge of God and His oneness, or the other attributes of His perfection, whether affirmative or negative, and from the knowledge of the angels, the messengers, the revealed books, and the Day of Resurrection. Many people have all of this knowledge without being believers. Satan himself knows all these things as well as you and I, and he is an unbeliever. Someone who acquires the knowledge of something by means of rational proof or conformity to religion must in addition submit to the object of that knowledge; he must bring about a state of surrender and humility, of acceptance and assent, in his heart in order to become a believer. The perfection of faith lies in tranquillity (*itmi'nan*), for once the light of faith has become strong, it will produce tranquillity in the heart. All of this is quite different from knowledge. It is possible that your intellect should perceive something by means of a rational proof, but until your heart has submitted that knowledge is of no use. For example, intellect enables you to understand that a dead person cannot harm you in any way, and indeed that all the dead in the world do not have as much capacity for sensation or motion as even a fly, for all faculties, corporeal and mental, have left them. But since you do not accept this in your heart, because your heart has not submitted to what your intellect tells you, you could not endure the darkness of a night spent in the company of a corpse. Were your heart to submit to your intellect and to accept its instruction, such a prospect would present no difficulty. If you applied yourself to the task, in the end you would have no fear of the dead.

It is thus apparent that submission, which is a quality pertaining to the heart, is different from knowledge, a quality pertaining to the intellect. It is entirely possible that someone should be able, by means of rational proof, to prove the existence of the Almighty Creator and His oneness, the Day of Resurrection, and all the other true doctrines. But proving the veracity of those doctrines does not constitute belief, and the one proving them does not count as a believer; he may be an unbeliever, a hypocrite, or a *mushrik*. Today your eye is closed and does not have the vision of the unseen; the corporeal eye is incapable of seeing. When innermost secrets are revealed and the true sovereignty of Allah manifests itself, when the natural realm is destroyed and reality becomes utterly clear, then you will become aware that you were not believers in God. The activity of the intellect has no connection to belief. Until *la ilaha illa 'llah* is inscribed by the pen of the intellect on the pure tablet of the heart, one is not a believer in God's oneness. And once that pure and sacred word has entered the heart, sovereignty over it belongs to God Almighty Himself;

you will not permit anyone to exert any influence on what has now become God's realm. You will not expect splendor or rank, seek fame or dignity, from anyone. The heart will then be fully purified of hypocrisy and pretense. So if you see any hypocrisy in your heart, know that your heart has not submitted to your intellect, that belief has not illumined your heart, that you have granted divinity to one other than God and regarded one other than Him as the source of effects in this world. You belong, therefore, to the category of the hypocrites, the *mushrikin* or the unbelievers.

LEGAL RULINGS ON THE DEFENSE OF THE ISLAMIC LANDS

These rulings are taken from Tahrir al-Wasila *(Najaf, 1390/1970, I, pp. 485-487), the systematic treatise on the specific ordinances of fiqh written by Imam Khomeini during the initial period of his exile, spent in the western Turkish city of Bursa. Although no Muslim country is mentioned in name, for the purpose is to provide rulings of general applicability, not specific to a given situation, it is plain that some rulings are inspired by the parlous situation in Iran and that others allude to the Zionist aggression against Palestine and other Muslim lands.*

If an enemy from whom harm is anticipated to Muslim land or society approaches the lands of the Muslims or their frontier regions, the areas in question must be defended by whatever means possible, including the expenditure of lives and property.

The foregoing is not conditional on the presence of the [Hidden] Imam, upon whom be peace, or upon his permission or that of his deputy, specifically named or collective. Defense is incumbent on all who are legally responsible (*mukallaf*) by whatever means are available, without any restriction or condition.

If there is fear of the Muslim lands being conquered, of such conquest being extended, or of the lands becoming [permanently] occupied and the Muslims being taken captive, defense is incumbent by whatever means possible.

If there is fear of the Muslim lands falling under political and economic domination leading to their political and economic enslavement and the weakening and enfeeblement of Islam and the Muslims, defense of Islam is incumbent by appropriate means, including passive resistance, commercial boycotts, and the severance of all dealings and relations.

If commercial or other relations are liable to endanger the Muslim lands through enabling foreigners to dominate them politically or otherwise, leading to their colonization, even in undeclared form, the maintenance of such relations is forbidden and must be avoided.

If political relations between the Islamic states and foreigners leads to the domination of the latter over the Muslim lands or over the persons and properties of the Muslims, it is forbidden for heads of state to maintain such relations. All obligations arising from such relations are void, and it is incumbent on the Muslims to instruct their leaders and compel them to abandon such relations, even if this involves passive resistance.

If there is a danger of attack by foreigners on one of the Islamic states, it is incumbent on all of them to come to its defense by whatever means possible, just as it is incumbent on the generality of the Muslims.

If one of the Islamic states signs a treaty providing for relations that are inimical to the interests of Islam and the Muslims, it is incumbent on the other states to remedy the situation by political and economic means, such as the severance of political and commercial relations. It is similarly incumbent on all Muslims to concern themselves with the matter to the extent possible by such means as passive resistance. All obligations arising from such relations are void according to the law of Islam.

If the head of an Islamic state or the member of a legislative assembly, in either its lower or upper house, facilitates or causes the acquisition by foreigners of political or economic influence over an Islamic country that threatens the integrity of the Islamic world or the independence of the country in question, in present or in the future, that person is a traitor and forfeits his position, whatever it may be, and even if he originally acquired it in legitimate fashion. It is the duty of the Islamic *ummah* to punish him, even if it be only to the extent of waging passive resistance and boycotting the individual in question in all possible ways. He should be excluded from all political activity and deprived of his social rights.

If commercial relations, undertaken by Muslim states or individuals, with foreign states or merchants threaten the market and livelihood of Muslims, such relations must be abandoned and the commerce resulting from them is illicit. It is incumbent on the Shi'i scholars (ru'asa' 'l-madhhab) to prohibit acquisition of the goods in question and trading in them, and it is incumbent on the Muslims to follow their directives in this respect.

A SPEECH GIVEN TO A
DELEGATION OF CUSTOMS OFFICIALS

Noteworthy in this address, given on March 27, 1979 to a delegation of customs officials visiting him soon after the triumph of the revolution but plainly intended for a wider audience, is the political interpretation Imam Khomeini gives to the Qur'anic concepts of "light" and "darkness." This interpretation is clearly not intended to be exhaustive, and is ultimately subordinate to the correlation of light with belief and darkness with unbelief contained in the first extract provided here. It was precisely in the Imam's vision of Islam as a seamless whole, with the inner and the outer, the spiritual and the political, closely interwoven, that his genius lay. Translated from Sahifa-yi Imam, *Tehran, 1378 Sh./1999, VII, pp. 135-138.*

"Allah is the Friend and Protector of those who believe; He brings them forth from darkness into light. As for the disbelievers, their friends and protectors are the evil ones (*al-taghut*); they bring them forth from light into darkness" (Qur'an, 2:258). Those who are with God, who are oriented to God and have faith in God, God will bring them forth from all types of darkness and convey them to the essence of light. Faith in God is light: faith in God causes all the darkness confronting the believers to dissipate; faith in God immerses the believers in the light of God. The darkness of despotism, the darkness of repression, the darkness of dependency, the darkness of injustice - believers are delivered from all these forms of darkness. People who are oriented to God, whose aim is a godly one, are delivered from all types of darkness - outer and inner - and are immersed in an ocean of light.

People of Iran, because you depended on your faith and oriented yourselves towards God, because as a single body you turned to Islam, desiring its implementation, God delivered you, and He will continue to deliver you. He delivered you from the great barrier of despotism; you shattered it, dispelled its darkness and entered the light of freedom. You shattered the barrier of dependency, thanks to your faith, and you entered the light of independence. You shattered the barriers of repression, and entered into true Islam, which is identical with light, for all other than Islam is darkness. By orienting yourselves to Islam, by orienting yourselves to the Imams, by orienting yourselves to the Qur'an, you were able to shatter all those barriers that people thought unbreakable, to defeat all those powers that people thought invincible. Worldly calculations proved false, the calculations of the materialists proved false.

According to the calculations of those who did not believe in God, it did not make sense that a people that had nothing should be able to triumph over a power that had everything. It did not make sense that such a people should be able to stop a foreign power, armed to the teeth with all kinds of weapons, from plundering its resources. Their calculations were entirely materialistic; based on conventional and material considerations, they thought it impossible that we should triumph. But they failed to take into account those spiritual factors which have always enabled Islam to advance. At the very beginning of Islam, although the Muslims had very little in the way of equipment - a single horse or a single sword to be shared among several people - they defeated the armies of Byzantium and Persia, with their soldiers armed to the teeth and many times more numerous than the Muslims; through the power of faith, they defeated the Byzantine Empire and the Persian Empire.

Soldiers of Islam, young men and believers! Through your faith you have shattered this great barrier, defeated the satanic forces of evil and tyranny. You have advanced thanks to your faith and disproved all the calculations of the materialists. God has granted you victory and He will continue to grant you victory, as long as you remain oriented to Him.

My dear brothers! Do not abandon this secret of your success, do not abandon orientation to God, to Islam. For the Muslim, for the believer, martyrdom is a source of happiness. Our young men regard martyrdom as a blessing, and this, too, is a secret of our success. People who are materialists or materialistically inclined never long for martyrdom, but our young men regard it as a blessing, a source of tranquillity. Those who thought that at the present juncture they could cause dissension among our dear young men are mistaken. Our young men are all oriented to Islam, and are all moving forward with a firm faith.

We still have a long way to go. All of us, all segments of the population, must together restore this ruin they have left behind. In the name of the "Great Civilization" they have uprooted every trace of civilization from Iran; in the name of "Land Reform" they have destroyed our agriculture. They have destroyed our educational system and made our army dependent on foreigners, They have weakened our nation and plundered our treasuries to live lives of luxury abroad. God willing we will recover from them what they have stolen.

These traitors have left behind a distressed and ruined country, a country where workers are poor, peasants are poor, shopkeepers are poor, a country where even on the outskirts of Tehran itself there are whole districts of miserable people living in caves! This is what they have left us.

There is no single segment of the population that by itself can restore this ruin to prosperity. The government can't; the religious scholars can't; the bazaaris can't; the peasants can't; the workers can't. But all of them together can do so, for "the hand of God is with the whole community." Only when all groups come together can tasks be achieved. You have seen how through unity of purpose, collaboration and trust in God you destroyed that great obstacle; now you must bring prosperity to this ruin using the same means.

You who serve on the borders of our country in the customs must do your part in this, as must those who serve in the capital and provincial centers. Don't expect the government to do everything, in just the same way that the government shouldn't expect the people to do everything. God willing, let us all work together, and move forward, for the same of Islam, for the sake of the Islamic Republic, for the sake of the laws of Islam.

And peace, blessings and the mercy of God be upon you.

Extracts from the Writings of Dr. Ali Shari'ati

THE TWO PERIODS OF SHI'ISM

This extract from Tashayyu'-i 'Alavi va Tashayyu'-i Safavi *(Tehran, 1350 Sh./1971, pp. 24-26) illustrates well several leading characteristics of Shari'ati's thought: his presentation of Shi'ism as being in its essence a revolutionary movement; his rejection of the cultural and devotional forms that allegedly came to distort it from the Safavid period onwards; and his delight in the use of binary oppositions taken from the vocabulary of sociology, often cited in the original French (here, "mouvement" and "institution.")*

Shi'ism has passed through two completely distinct and separate periods. One period begins with the first Islamic century and ends with the beginning of the Safavid dynasty. During this period Shi'ism was an expression of Islam as "movement" as opposed to the Islam of the ruling institution, i.e., the caliphate; it was the period of vitality and movement. The other period began with the Safavids and continues until today; it is the period in which Shi'ism as a movement has been transformed into Shi'ism as an institution.

The early Shi'a were a minority, ruled by others and lacking all power. They were not able to go freely to Karbala, they were not able to mention the name of [Imam] Husayn, and they were not able even to perform their religious rituals in front of others. They were always persecuted, always being tortured or in prison, or hiding in *taqiya*.[1] Then [under the Safavids] those selfsame Shi'a were transformed into a great power ruling a country where they enjoyed the maximum protection of the powers-that-be. The same pole[2] that used to oppress the Shi'a and would arrest, torture and kill people for the crime of loving [Imam] 'Ali, now begins to call itself "a dog at the threshold of [Imam] Reza."[3] What a great triumph!

The same ruler who for nine hundred years had been persecuting the Shi'a now hangs his boots around his neck and makes a pilgrimage on foot from Isfahan to Mashhad! Yes, on foot! What a great triumph![4]

The same ruler who for ten centuries regularly prevented people from visiting the graves of the Imams, who cut off the water supplies to the shrines and destroyed them, now covers the domes over those tombs with gold, provides those tombs with silver railings, and decorates the minarets with faience tiles! What a great triumph!

The pilgrimage that the ardent Shi'i would undertake to Mashhad or Karbala, enduring manifold dangers and difficulties

---

[1] This is a highly oversimplified depiction of the Shi'a predicament in pre-Safavid times. The features mentioned by Shari'ati are by no means absent from the historical picture, but did not characterize every age and every place. *Taqiya*: the prudential dissimulation of one's Shi'i identity in circumstances of presumed danger to oneself or the community.

[2] By "pole" Shari'ati means the oppressive power of the state that has throughout history stood over against the other "pole," the oppressed and deprived masses.

[3] An allusion to the only apparently self-deprecatory title assumed by Shah 'Abbas I, one of the Safavid rulers.

[4] Another allusion to Shah 'Abbas, who undertook the pilgrimage in question in 1601. He is not of course "the same ruler" who persecuted the Shi'a for centuries; it is simply that from Shari'ati's point of view he is indistinguishable from all the rulers who preceded him, despite his profession of Shi'ism.

at the hands of the government, is now proclaimed by that same government to be an official religious pilgrimage, similar or even equivalent to the Hajj![5] The government gave the pilgrim returning from Mashhad or Karbala the title of "Mashhadi" or "Karbala'i," just as the pilgrim returning from Mecca is known as Hajji![6] What a great triumph!

Those same Shi'i scholars and clerics who were always in the front ranks of the struggle against various governments, who were constantly the targets on which the arrows of the ruling institution rained down, now begin living under the most splendid and luxurious of circumstances! They sit next to the ruler and are consulted by him on matters of state! In fact, the ruler considers his power to have been bestowed on him by the Shi'i scholars who are the deputies of the [Twelfth] Imam and the legitimate rulers [hakim-i shar']! They have assigned rulership to him by virtue of their deputyship! What a great triumph![7]

It is precisely when Shi'ism begins to achieve all these triumphs that it is defeated. Once all the obstacles to the performance of its religious rituals, all the barriers to the expression of its sentiments, are removed; once the factors that used to oppress it begin to encourage it and conform to it - then Shi'ism stops advancing, and it is transformed into a social institution, a ruling power!

This is how the law for the transformation of a movement into an institution operates. A fervent belief which once agitated for dynamic, revolutionary change in all dimensions of society is transformed into an institution! It becomes one of the fixed, official bases of society; it merges with and adjusts itself to the other bases of society; it becomes one institution among others, like the state, the family, or language, or [worse still], like insurance, a bank, a pension, a savings account, a lottery ticket!

---

5 Here Shari'ati is alluding once again to Shah 'Abbas who, alarmed by the amounts of gold being taken out of the country by pilgrims making the Hajj, sought to promote pilgrimage to Mashhad as a patriotic substitute.

6 The entry into currency of the titles "Mashhadi" and "Karbala'i" seems to have been the result of popular usage, not governmental decree.

7 Here the allusion is presumably to proclamations made by Shaykh 'Ali Karaki with respect to Shah Tahmasp, the second Safavid ruler.

TAWHID, AS MANIFESTED IN THE HAJJ, THE CURE FOR ALIENATION

Taken from Islamshinasi *(Tehran, n.d., pp. 422-424), Shari'ati's lengthiest and most nearly systematic exposition of his ideas, this extract exemplifies his disdain for tradional modes of analysis and his preference for a vigorous and emotive language that draws in large part on concepts current in the leftist discourse of the 1960's and 1970's (e.g., "alienation, "ideological superstructure.") The unquestionably powerful insight that the Hajj is a vast, practical manifestation of* tauhid *was developed by him in detail in another work quite simply entitled* Hajj.

How can man, alienated from himself, bewitched by money, power, the machine, *shirk*, illusion, class, race, tyranny, the institutions governing life — how can man, turned into a wolf or a fox, a mouse or a sheep, alienated from this world and the next, man who has ceased being man in every respect, who has become a stranger to himself — how can he rediscover himself, how can he return to his primordial and essential being, and become himself once again?

My answer is simple: by means of *tawhid*. But *tawhid* understood as a concept of infinite scope, heavily laden with meanings and wonders, a word as weighty, rich and substantial as the entirety of existence. Mere words are, in fact, incapable of sustaining the weight of *tawhid*, and the tongue is too lowly to express it without rendering it deficient, superficial and poor.

It may be precisely for this reason that the tongue of revelation, being obliged to use human vocabulary, has preferred to express tawhid by means of a series of movements, not by means of words — *tawhid* with all of its basic concepts, each one of which has in turn hundreds of different manifestations, *tawhid* the rays of which shine on every feeling and sensation.

Each of those movements is a symbol, a symbol that has far greater capacity than mere speech for conveying meaning and emotion, and for giving inspiration to man's senses and perception.

Thus it is that *tawhid* becomes objectively manifest, on a single great natural stage, provided by mountains, valleys, and plains, in the most simple and majestic form, by means of orderly, coherent movements that are bound up with time itself. It manifests itself in all four of its dimensions - worldview, history, sociology, anthropology -- as ideological superstructure and ultimate goal of existence and purpose of man's being. In order to understand *tawhid*, the pupil must experience it with all of his spirit and body, he must feel it in his thoughts and his feelings, his skin and his flesh.

Where does this take place?

On the Hajj!

Index

61,000
12,000   1 year
─────────
49 000
12,000   2 years
─────────
37, 000
12, 000   3 years
─────────
25 000
12, 000   4 years
─────────
13, 000   5 years
13, 000
─────────

Boga   250 − unu   84
Boga 4⟌1000   5
Chase   8   ─────
mulupluyo   20/30   89 unguddt

30,000
  .08
────────
2400 000
─────────
$2,400 TAX
3,000 at least +

Matt ~~~~~
1299 Bush St.
#404
San Francisco, CA
94109

MIZAN PUBLICATIONS
available from
ISLAMIC PUBLICATIONS INTERNATIONAL

On the Sociology of Islam by Ali Shari'ati tr. by Hamid Algar
Paperback ISBN 0-933782-00-4 $ 9.95

Marxism and Other Western Fallacies: An Islamic Critique by Ali Shari'ati
tr. Robert Campbell
Paperback ISBN 0-933782-06-3 $ 9.95 Hardback ISBN 0-933782-05-5 $ 19.95

Constitution of the Islamic Republic of Iran tr. Hamid Algar
Paperback ISBN 0-933782-07-1 $ 4.95 Hardback ISBN 0-933782-02-0 $ 14.95

Islam and Revolution: Writings and Declaration of Imam Khomeini
tr. Hamid Algar
Paperback ISBN 0-933782-03-9 $ 19.95 Hardback ISBN 0-933782-04-7 $ 29.95

The Islamic Struggle in Syria by Umar F. Abd-Allah
Hardback ISBN 0-933782-10-1 $ 29.95

Occidentosis: A Plaque from the West by Jalal Al-i Ahmad tr. Robert Campbell
Paperback ISBN 0-933782-13-6 $ 9.95 Hardback ISBN 0-933782-12-8 $ 19.95

The Contemporary Muslim Movement in the Philippines by Cesar Adib Majul
Paperback ISBN 0-933782-17-9 $ 9.95 Hardback ISBN 0-933782-16-9 $ 19.95

Fundamental of Islamic Thought: God, Man and the Universe
by Ayatullah Murtaza Mutahhari tr. Robert Campbell
Paperback ISBN 0-933782-15-2 $ 9.95

Social and Historical Change: An Islamic Perspective
by Ayatullah Murtaza Mutahhari tr. by Robert Campbell
Paperback ISBN 0-933782-19-5 $ 9.95 Hardback ISBN 0-933782-18-7 $ 19.95

Principles of Sufism by Al-Qushayri tr. B. R. Von Schlegell
Paperback ISBN 0-933782-20-9 $ 19.95 Hardback ISBN 0-933782-21-7 $ 29.95

Also available are the following Islamic Book Trust publications:

Modern Islamic Political Thought by Hamid Enyat, Foreword by Hamid Algar
Paperback ISBN 983-9154-15-X $ 24.95

The Qur'anic Phenomenon by Malik Bennabi
tr. by Mohamed el-Tahir el-Mesawi Paperback ISBN 983-9154-25-7 $ 24.95

Ghazali and Prayer by Kojiro Nakamura
Paperback ISBN 983-9154-36-2 $ 24.95

8/02

Also published by

ISLAMIC PUBLICATIONS INTERNATIONAL

Surat Al-Fatiha: Foundation of the Qur'an by Hamid Algar
Paperback ISBN 1-889999-00-8 $ 5.95

Sufism: Principles and Practice by Hamid Algar
Paperback ISBN 1-889999-02-4 $ 5.95

Jesus In The Qur'an: His Reality Expounded in the Qur'an by Hamid Algar
Paperback ISBN 1-889999-09-1 $ 5.95

Understanding The Four Madhhabs: The Facts about Ijtihad and Taqlid
by Abdal Hakim Murad (T.J. Winters)
Paperback ISBN 1-889999-07-5 $ 3.00

The Sunnah: Its Obligatory and Exemplary Aspects by Hamid Algar
Paperback ISBN 1-889999-01-6 $ 5.95

Imam Abu Hamid Ghazali: An Exponent of Islam in Its Totality
by Hamid Algar
Paperback ISBN 1-889999-15-6 $ 5.95

Hasan Al-Banna: Founder of the First Modern Islamic Movement
by Hamid Algar
Paperback ISBN # 1-889999-18-0 $ 7.95

Wahhabism: Origins and Doctrines by Hamid Algar
Paperback ISBN # 1-889999-13-X $ 7.95

Social Justice in Islam by Sayyid Qutb
Translation Revised and Introduction by Hamid Algar
Paperback ISBN # 1-889999-11-3 $ 19.95
Hardback ISBN # 1-889999-12-1 $ 29.95

Sales Tax: Please add 7% for books shipped to New York address.
Shipping: $4.00 for the first book and $ 1.00 for additional publication